Teach Yourself
VISUALLY™

Word® 2003
2nd Edition

Visual

by Elaine Marmel

WILEY

Wiley Publishing, Inc.

Teach Yourself VISUALLY™ Word® 2003
2nd Edition

Published by
Wiley Publishing, Inc.
111 River Street
Hoboken, NJ 07030-5774

Published simultaneously in Canada

Copyright © 2006 by Wiley Publishing, Inc., Indianapolis, Indiana

Library of Congress Control Number: 2005938173

ISBN-13: 978-0-471-78488-3
ISBN-10: 0-471-78488-5
Manufactured in the United States of America

10 9 8 7 6 5 4 3 2 1

Trademark Acknowledgments

Contact Us

For general information on our other products and services please contact our Customer Care Department within the U.S. at 800-762-2974, outside the U.S. at 317-572-3993 or fax 317-572-4002.

For technical support please visit www.wiley.com/techsupport.

Wiley Publishing, Inc.

Sales

Contact Wiley
at (800) 762-2974 or
fax (317) 572-4002.

Praise for Visual Books

"Like a lot of other people, I understand things best when I see them visually. Your books really make learning easy and life more fun."

John T. Frey (Cadillac, MI)

"I have quite a few of your Visual books and have been very pleased with all of them. I love the way the lessons are presented!"

Mary Jane Newman (Yorba Linda, CA)

"I just purchased my third Visual book (my first two are dog-eared now!), and, once again, your product has surpassed my expectations.

Tracey Moore (Memphis, TN)

"I am an avid fan of your Visual books. If I need to learn anything, I just buy one of your books and learn the topic in no time. Wonders! I have even trained my friends to give me Visual books as gifts."

Illona Bergstrom (Aventura, FL)

"Thank you for making it so clear. I appreciate it. I will buy many more Visual books."

J.P. Sangdong (North York, Ontario, Canada)

"I have several books from the Visual series and have always found them to be valuable resources."

Stephen P. Miller (Ballston Spa, NY)

"Thank you for the wonderful books you produce. It wasn't until I was an adult that I discovered how I learn – visually. Nothing compares to Visual books. I love the simple layout. I can just grab a book and use it at my computer, lesson by lesson. And I understand the material! You really know the way I think and learn. Thanks so much!"

Stacey Han (Avondale, AZ)

"I absolutely admire your company's work. Your books are terrific. The format is perfect, especially for visual learners like me. Keep them coming!"

Frederick A. Taylor, Jr. (New Port Richey, FL)

"I have several of your Visual books and they are the best I have ever used."

Stanley Clark (Crawfordville, FL)

"I bought my first Teach Yourself VISUALLY book last month. Wow. Now I want to learn everything in this easy format!"

Tom Vial (New York, NY)

"Thank you, thank you, thank you...for making it so easy for me to break into this high-tech world. I now own four of your books. I recommend them to anyone who is a beginner like myself."

Gay O'Donnell (Calgary, Alberta, Canada)

"I write to extend my thanks and appreciation for your books. They are clear, easy to follow, and straight to the point. Keep up the good work! I bought several of your books and they are just right! No regrets! I will always buy your books because they are the best."

Seward Kollie (Dakar, Senegal)

"Compliments to the chef!! Your books are extraordinary! Or, simply put, extra-ordinary, meaning way above the rest! THANK YOU THANK YOU THANK YOU! I buy them for friends, family, and colleagues."

Christine J. Manfrin (Castle Rock, CO)

"What fantastic teaching books you have produced! Congratulations to you and your staff. You deserve the Nobel Prize in Education in the Software category. Thanks for helping me understand computers."

Bruno Tonon (Melbourne, Australia)

"Over time, I have bought a number of your 'Read Less - Learn More' books. For me, they are THE way to learn anything easily. I learn easiest using your method of teaching."

José A. Mazón (Cuba, NY)

"I am an avid purchaser and reader of the Visual series, and they are the greatest computer books I've seen. The Visual books are perfect for people like myself who enjoy the computer, but want to know how to use it more efficiently. Your books have definitely given me a greater understanding of my computer, and have taught me to use it more effectively. Thank you very much for the hard work, effort, and dedication that you put into this series."

Alex Diaz (Las Vegas, NV)

Credits

Project Editor
Maureen Spears

Acquisitions Editor
Jody Lefevere

**Product Development
Manager**
Courtney Allen

Copy Editor
Lauren Kennedy

Technical Editor
Daniel Hodge

Editorial Manager
Robyn Siesky

Manufacturing
Allan Conley
Linda Cook
Paul Gilchrist
Jennifer Guynn

Book Design
Kathie Rickard

Production Coordinator
Maridee Ennis

Layout
Jennifer Heleine
Amanda Spagnuolo

Screen Artist
Jill A. Proll

Illustrators
Steve Amory
Matthew Bell
Elizabeth Cardenas-Nelson
Ronda David-Burroughs
Cheryl Grubbs
Jake Mansfield
Rita Marley
Paul Schmitt

Proofreader
Vicki Broyles

Quality Control
Joe Niesen
Leeann Harney

Indexer
Ty Koontz

Special Help
Adrienne Porter

**Vice President and Executive
Group Publisher**
Richard Swadley

Vice President and Publisher
Barry Pruett

Composition Director
Debbie Stailey

About the Author

Elaine Marmel is president of Marmel Enterprises, LLC, an organization that specializes in freelance technical writing and software training. Elaine has an MBA from Cornell University and has worked on projects to build financial management systems in New York City and Washington, D.C. Elaine spends most of her time writing; since 1994, she has been a contributing editor to monthly magazines *Peachtree Extra* and *QuickBooks Extra*. She cowrote *Peachtree For Dummies* (Wiley, 2004), and wrote *Microsoft Office Project 2003 Bible* (Wiley, 2003), *Master VISUALLY Project 2003* (Wiley, 2004), and *Master VISUALLY QuickBooks 2005* (Wiley, 2005), and she has authored and coauthored more than 30 other books.

Although a native of Chicago, Elaine has seen much of the world, including Cincinnati, Ohio; Jerusalem, Israel; Ithaca, New York; Washington, D.C., and Tampa, FL. As of this writing, she has settled into a perfect house in Arizona, and lives with her purrfect cats, Cato, Watson, and Buddy (who seems to be made of velcro, sticking to Elaine when she starts to write), and her doting and loving dog, Josh (who watches the door for visitors and may lick you to death while performing the job of general welcoming committee).

Author's Acknowledgments

Special thanks go to Acquisitions Editor Jody Lefevere, to project editor Maureen Spears, to copy editor Lauren Kennedy, to technical editor Daniel Hodge, and finally to the graphics and production teams at Wiley.

Dedication

To Gayle Kearney, a true friend.

Table of Contents

 **A First Look at Word**

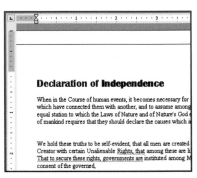

chapter 2 **Managing Documents**

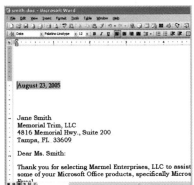

chapter**3**   **Edit Text**

Table of Contents

chapter 4 Proofreading

chapter 5 Format Text

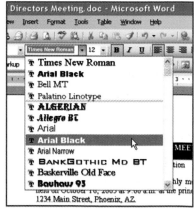

chapter 6

Format Paragraphs

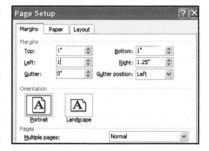

chapter 7

Format Pages

Table of Contents

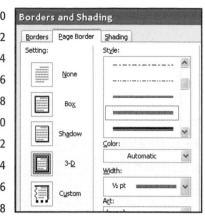

chapter 8 Print Documents

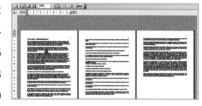

chapter 9 Work with Tables

chapter **10**   **Work with Graphics**

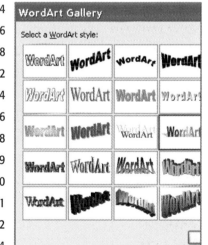

Table of Contents

Customize Word

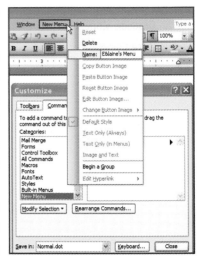

Work with Mass Mailing Tools

chapter 13 Work with Speech Recognition

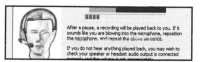

chapter 14 Word and the Internet

How to use this book

How to Use this Teach Yourself VISUALLY Book

Do you look at the pictures in a book or newspaper before anything else on a page? Would you rather see an image instead of read about how to do something? Search no further. This book is for you. Opening *Teach Yourself VISUALLY Word 2003* allows you to read less and learn more about the Word program.

Who Needs This Book

This book is for a reader who has never used this particular technology or software application. It is also for more computer literate individuals who want to expand their knowledge of the different features that Word has to offer.

Book Organization

Teach Yourself VISUALLY Word 2003 has 14 chapters.

Chapter 1, **A First Look at Word**, covers Word basics, including an overview of the Word Window, how to enter text, and how to use the menus, toolbars, and task panes.

Chapter 2, **Manage Documents**, shows you how to save, compare, switch between, and search a document.

In Chapter 3, **Edit Text**, you learn how to insert, edit, delete, move, and translate text as well as how to view it in various views and magnifications.

In Chapter 4, **Proofreading**, you find out how to find and replace text, correct mistakes, track changes and more.

Chapter 5, **Format Text**, shows you how to change fonts, and text size, color, and case. You also discover the finer points of formatting text.

Chapter 6, **Format Paragraphs**, covers text alignment, line spacing, bulleted and numbered lists, tabs, indented paragraphs, and how to work with styles.

In Chapter 7, **Format Pages**, you find out how to insert page and section breaks, number lines and pages, generate a table of contents, apply a theme, and use headers, footers, and footnotes.

Chapter 8, **Print Documents**, shows you how to print a document, labels, and envelopes and how to preview a document before you print it.

In Chapter 9, **Work with Tables**, you organize text quickly by creating a table and then changing its various elements to present your information in the most accessible format.

Chapter 10, **Work with Graphics**, introduces features such as WordArt, clip art, AutoShapes, text boxes, and more. You also discover how to change the appearance of your graphics and how to create a diagram.

In Chapter 11, **Customize Word**, you discover how to display formatting information and create and customize toolbars and menus, as well as how to create and run a macro.

Chapter 12, **Work with Mass Mailing Tools**, explains how to create mass mailings of letters and labels.

Chapter 13, **Using Speech Recognition**, shows you how to set up and use speech recognition.

In Chapter 14, **Word and the Internet**, you learn how to e-mail documents, create hyperlinks, and how to save a document as a Web page.

Chapter Organization

This book consists of sections, all listed in the book's table of contents. A *section* is a set of steps that show you how to complete a specific computer task.

Each section, usually contained on two facing pages, has an introduction to the task at hand, a set of full-color screen shots and steps that walk you through the task, and a set of tips. This format enables you to quickly look at a topic of interest and learn it instantly.

Chapters group together three or more sections with a common theme. A chapter may also contain pages that give you the background information you need to understand the sections in a chapter.

What You Need to Use This Book

To perform the steps in this book, you need the following:

● A personal computer with a 233-MHz or faster processor

● 128MB of RAM or more

● 350MB of hard disk space to install Word 2003

● A CD-ROM or DVD drive

● A Super VGA monitor (800 x 600 resolution or higher) and 256 colors

● Microsoft Windows XP or Windows 2000 with Service Pack 3

● An Internet connection

● A microphone (nothing expensive)

Using the Mouse

This book uses the following conventions to describe the actions you perform when using the mouse:

Click

Press your left mouse button once. You generally click your mouse on something to select something on the screen.

Double-click

Press your left mouse button twice. Double-clicking something on the computer screen generally opens whatever item you have double-clicked.

Right-click

Press your right mouse button. When you right-click anything on the computer screen, the program displays a shortcut menu containing commands specific to the selected item.

Click and Drag, and Release the Mouse

Move your mouse pointer and hover it over an item on the screen. Press and hold down the left mouse button. Now, move the mouse to where you want to place the item and then release the button. You use this method to move an item from one area of the computer screen to another.

The Conventions in This Book

A number of typographic and layout styles have been used throughout *Teach Yourself VISUALLY Word 2003* to distinguish different types of information.

Bold

Bold type represents the names of commands and options that you interact with. Bold type also indicates text and numbers that you must type into a dialog box or window.

Italics

Italic words introduce a new term and are followed by a definition.

Numbered Steps

You must perform the instructions in numbered steps in order to successfully complete a section and achieve the final results.

Bulleted Steps

These steps point out various optional features. You do not have to perform these steps; they simply give additional information about a feature.

Indented Text

Indented text tells you what the program does in response to you following a numbered step. For example, if you click a certain menu command, a dialog box may appear, or a window may open. Indented text may also tell you what the final result is when you follow a set of numbered steps.

Notes

Notes give additional information. They may describe special conditions that may occur during an operation. They may warn you of a situation that you want to avoid; for example, the loss of data. A note may also cross-reference a related area of the book. A cross-reference may guide you to another chapter, or another section with the current chapter.

Icons and Buttons

Icons and buttons are graphical representations within the text. They show you exactly what you need to click to perform a step.

 You can easily identify the tips in any section by looking for the TIPS icon. Tips offer additional information, including tips, hints, and tricks. You can use the TIPS information to go beyond what you have learn learned in the steps.

Operating System Difference

The figures and steps in this book depict the Windows XP operating system. If you are using Windows 2000, your own screens may look different. Word 2003 does not work on earlier versions of the Windows operating system.

A First Look at Word

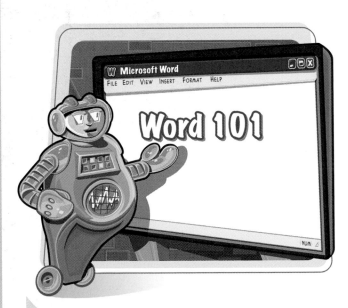

Word 101

Are you ready to get started in Word? In this first chapter, you become familiar with the Word working environment and you learn basic ways to navigate and to enter text.

You can open Microsoft Word a number of ways. This section demonstrates how to open Microsoft Word from the All Programs menu. Once Word opens, a blank document, ready for you to type text, appears.

Open Word

① Click **start**.

② Click **All Programs**.

③ Click **Microsoft Office**.

④ Click **Microsoft Office Word 2003**.

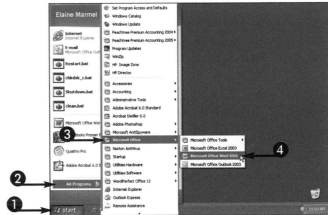

A blank document appears in the Word window.

● A button representing the document appears in the Windows Taskbar.

● To close Word, click the **Close** icon (⊠).

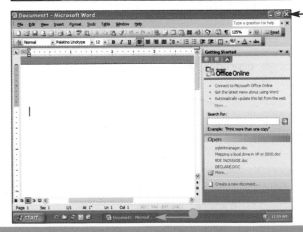

The Word window contains tools you can use to work quickly and efficiently while you are creating documents.

Title Bar
Shows the program and document titles.

Menu Bar
Shows menus that contain program commands. Also a box in which you can type a question for help.

Standard Toolbar
Contains buttons that open common actions, such as opening an existing document or creating a new document.

Formatting Toolbar
Contains buttons that perform common formatting actions, such as changing the font style or applying bold or italics.

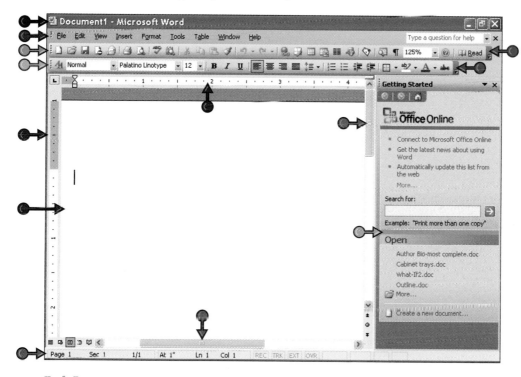

Toolbar Options Button
Displays buttons not visible on a toolbar due to insufficient screen space.

Rulers
Determines the physical location of text horizontally and vertically in relation to the margins. You can also set tab stops with the horizontal ruler and margins using either ruler.

Document Area
The area where you type. The flashing insertion point represents the location where text will appear when you type.

Task Pane
Displays common tasks. Its content changes, depending on the work you perform.

Scroll Bars
Reposition the document window horizontally or vertically. Drag the scroll boxes within the scroll bars or click the scroll bar arrows (🔼 and 🔽).

Status Bar
Displays information about the document and the location of the insertion point. From left to right, this bar contains: the Page area with the number of the page at the insertion point; the Sec area, with the number of the section at the insertion point; the 1/1 area, which gives the number of the page at the insertion point over the total document pages; the At area, which is the location of the insertion point vertically on the page in inches; the Ln area, which gives the line number at the insertion point, measured from the top margin; and the Col area, which shows the position within a line of the insertion point.

Enter Text

Word makes typing easy: You do not need to press Enter to start a new line. Word calculates when a new line should begin and automatically starts it for you.

When you type, you should use the Tab key instead of the Spacebar to add more than one space between words. See Chapter 6 for details on setting tabs.

Enter Text

TYPE TEXT

① Type the text that you want to appear in your document.

The text appears to the left of the insertion point as you type.

As the insertion point reaches the end of the line, Word automatically starts a new one.

Press **Enter** only to start a new paragraph.

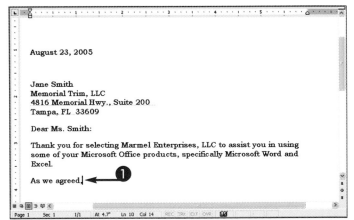

SEPARATE INFORMATION

① Type a word or phrase.

② Press **Tab**.

● To align text properly, press **Tab** to include more than one space between words.

Several spaces appear between the last letter you typed and the insertion point.

③ Type another word or phrase.

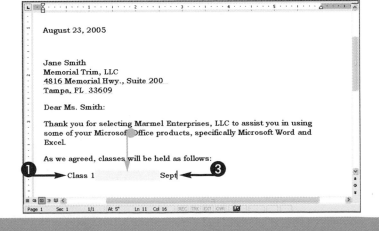

ENTER TEXT AUTOMATICALLY

1 Begin typing a common word, phrase, or date.

The AutoComplete feature suggests common words and phrases based on what you type.

● Word suggests the rest of the word, phrase, or month.

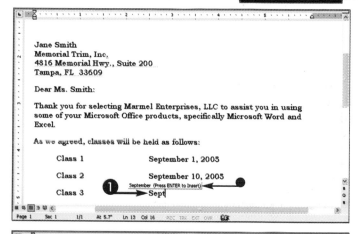

● You can press **Enter** to let Word finish typing the word, phrase, or month for you.

You can keep typing to ignore Word's suggestion.

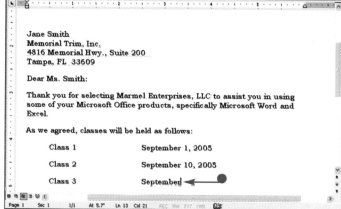

 TIP

Why should I use **Tab** instead of **Spacebar** to include more than one space between words?

Typically, when you include more than one space between words or phrases, you intend to align text in a columnar fashion. Most fonts are proportional, meaning each character of a font takes up a different amount of space on a line. Therefore, you cannot calculate the number of spaces needed to align words beneath each other. Tabs, however, are set at specific locations on a line, such as 3 inches. When you press **Tab**, you know exactly where words or phrases will appear on a line. Word sets default tabs every .5 inch; to avoid pressing **Tab** multiple times to separate text, change the tab settings.

Move Around in a Document

You can use many different techniques to move to a different location in a document; the technique you select depends on the location to which you want to move.

On to page 2

MOVE ONE CHARACTER

1 Note the location of the insertion point.

2 Press ➡.

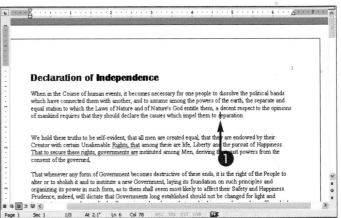

● Word moves the insertion point one character to the right.

You can press ⬅, ⬆, or ⬇ to move the insertion point one character left, up, or down.

Holding any arrow key moves the insertion point repeatedly in the direction of the arrow key.

You can press Ctrl + ➡ or Ctrl + ⬅ to move the insertion point one word at a time to the right or left.

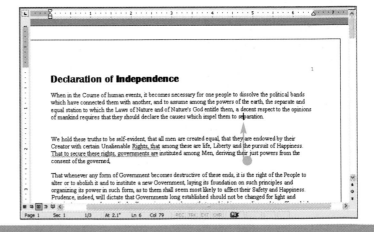

MOVE ONE SCREEN

1 Note the last visible line on-screen.

2 Press `Page Down`.

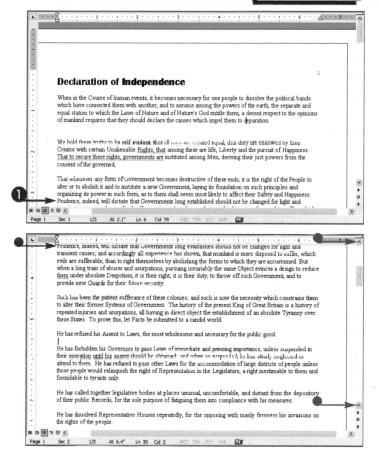

● Word moves the insertion point down one screen.

You can press `Page Up` to move the insertion point up one screen.

● You can click the **Tiles** icon (▲) to scroll up, or the **Icons** icon (▼) to scroll down, one line at a time in a document.

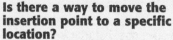

TIPS

Is there a way to quickly move the insertion point to the beginning or the end of a document?

Yes. Press `Ctrl`+`Home` to move the insertion point to the beginning of a document or `Ctrl`+`End` to move the insertion point to the bottom of a document. You can press `Shift`+`F5` to move the insertion point to the last place you changed in your document.

Is there a way to move the insertion point to a specific location?

Yes, you can use bookmarks to mark a particular place and then return to it. See Chapter 3 for details on creating a bookmark and returning to the bookmark's location. See Chapter 4 for details on searching for a specific word and, if necessary, replacing that word with a different one.

Using Menus

For your convenience, Word's menus list the actions — commands — you can take while using the program. Initially, the most commonly used commands appear. If you wait, Word expands the menu to display all commands. Or, you can expand the menu.

Word monitors the way you work and, over time, the commands you use most frequently appear on the menus.

Using Menus

1 Click a menu.

The menu opens, displaying the most commonly used commands.

2 Click the arrow at the bottom of the menu (▼).

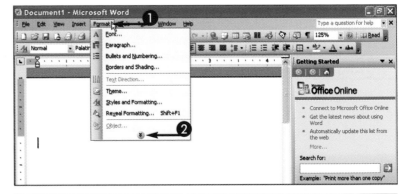

The menu expands to display the other commands available on the menu.

3 Click the command you want to use.

Note: Commands that appear gray are not currently available.

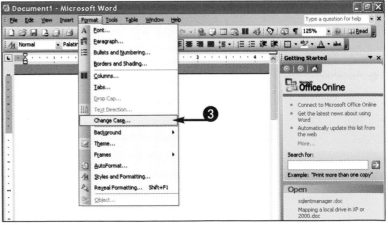

You can use toolbars, in addition to menus, to select commands. Toolbar buttons provide shortcuts to the same commands you can select on menus.

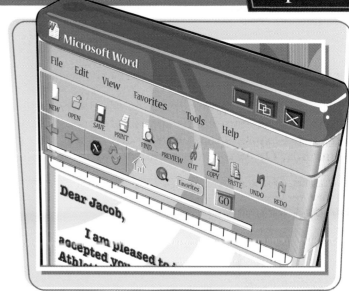

Using Toolbars

① Move the mouse pointer so that it points at a toolbar button.

● A ScreenTip appears in a yellow box, identifying the button's name and function.

You can click a button to perform its command.

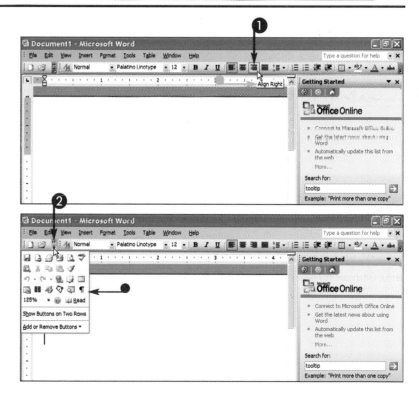

② Because not all buttons on a toolbar are visible, to display additional buttons, click the **Toolbar Options** icon (▤).

● Additional toolbar buttons appear.

Using the Task Pane

The task pane appears automatically on the right side of the Word screen to help you perform common tasks, such as opening new or recently used documents, searching for clip art, or applying styles to text.

Word contains several different task panes. The Getting Started task pane appears each time you start Word. You can switch to different task panes or let Word display them automatically when appropriate.

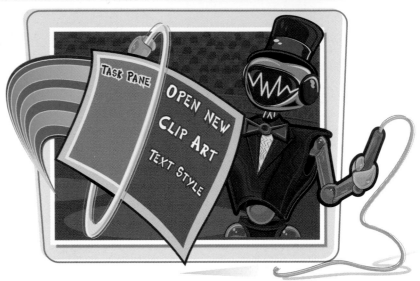

Using the Task Pane

HIDE THE TASK PANE

① Click the **Task Pane Close** icon (☒).

The task pane disappears.

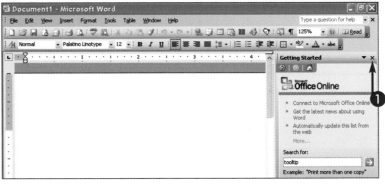

REDISPLAY THE TASK PANE

② Click **View**.

③ Click **Task Pane**.

The task pane appears.

Note: *When a check (☑) appears beside Task Pane on the View menu, the task pane is visible on-screen. When no check appears, the task pane is not visible.*

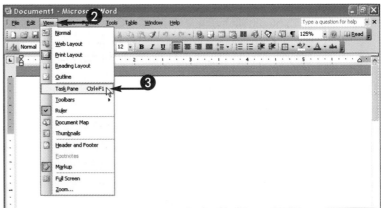

SWITCH TASK PANES

① Click the Getting Started ⏷.

Word displays a list of available task panes.

● A check ☑ appears beside the currently selected task pane.

② Click a task pane.

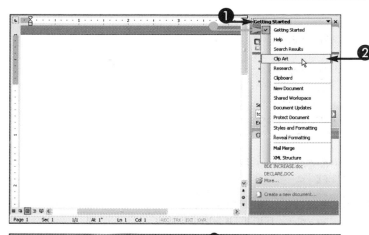

The new task pane appears.

● Each task pane's title appears here.

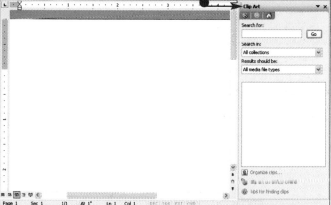

TIP

Can I stop the task pane from appearing when I start Word?

Yes. In the Options dialog box, which you open by clicking **Tools**, and then **Options**, do the following:

① Click the **View** tab.

② Click **Startup Task Pane** (☐ changes to ☑).

③ Click **OK**.

When you close and restart Word, the task pane does not appear.

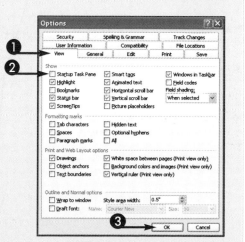

You can search for help with the Word tasks you perform. By default, Word searches the Help file on your computer as well as the Internet.

1 Click here and type a word or phrase related to the help topic you want to view.

2 Press **Enter**.

Help topics related to the word or phrase you typed appear in the task pane.

3 Click the topic most closely related to the subject on which you want help.

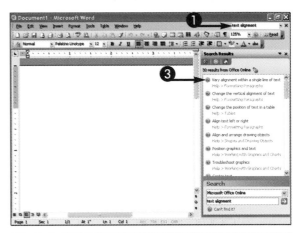

A new window containing the Help topic information opens beside the Word window.

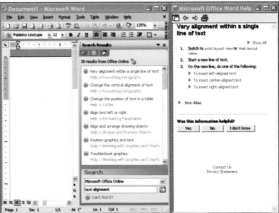

● You can display additional information for any line preceded by a carat if you click that line.

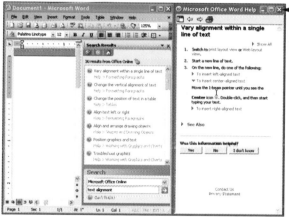

④ To close the Help window, click ⊠.

The Word window re-expands to fill the screen and the Search task pane containing the Help topics remains visible.

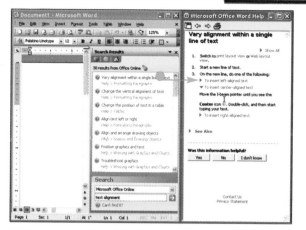

Can I make Word search only the Help file on my computer for topics instead of searching the Internet?

Yes. In the Search task pane, click the **Search** ⊡ and select **Offline Help**.

What do the different icons beside Help topics in the Search Results task pane mean?

Some of the most common icons are the **Help on Microsoft Online** icon (▣), which actually represents a Help topic in the file stored on your computer; the **Template on Microsoft Online** icon (▣), which represents a predefined template you can download to help you accomplish a task; **the Article on Microsoft Online** icon (▣), which represents a Web-based article containing helpful information; and the **Training on Microsoft Online** icon (▣), which represents a link to Internet training on the topic.

Managing Documents

Now that you know the basics, it is time to discover how to efficiently navigate among Word documents. In this chapter, you learn how to manage the Word documents you create.

Save
Documents

You can save documents so that you can use them at another time in Microsoft Word, or in another format so that you can share them with people who do not use Microsoft Word 2003.

SAVE IN MICROSOFT WORD FORMAT

1 Click **File**.

2 Click **Save**.

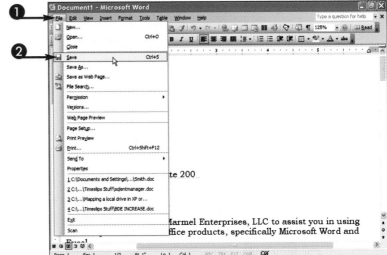

The Save As dialog box appears.

3 Type a name for the document here.

● You can click the **Save in** list ⬇ to select a location on your computer in which to save the document.

● The files and folders stored in the folder shown in the Save in list appear here.

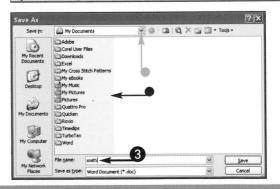

- You can click any of these buttons to navigate quickly to common locations to save documents.

- You can click the **Folder** icon (🗀) to create a new folder in which to store the document.

- You can click the **Views** icon (🔲▾) to change the view of files and folders.

④ Click **Save**.

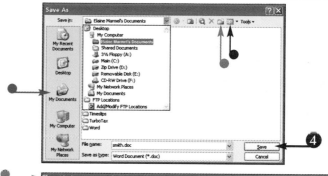

- Word saves the document and displays the name you supplied in the title bar.

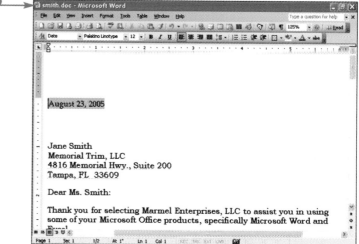

TIP

What views for files and folders can I select?

When you click 🔲▾, the list of available views appears.

Icon Name	Icon	Description
Thumbnails		Displays each file as a miniature picture, with the file name below the file.
Tiles		Displays icons for files in two columns; file names and sizes appear beside each file.
Icons		Displays a Word icon for each file, with the file name below the file.
List		Lists file names.
Details		Lists the file name, size, type, and date and time last modified.
Properties		Lists files on the left; when you select a file, statistics such as the editing time and creation date appear on the right.
Preview		Displays file names on the left; when you select a file, a preview of the document appears **on the right**.

continued

You also can save documents you create in Microsoft Word in a variety of other formats, such as Word templates, Web pages, or text files.

You also can save documents for use in older versions of Word or in Microsoft Works.

SAVE TO ANOTHER FORMAT

1 Click **File**.

2 Click **Save As**.

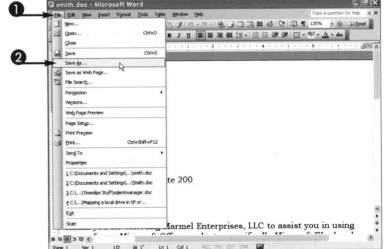

The Save As dialog box appears.

3 Type a name for the document.

● You can click here to navigate to a different folder in which to store the file.

● You can click any of these buttons to navigate quickly to common locations to save documents.

④ Click the **Save as type** ⬇.

Word displays the formats available for the document.

⑤ Click to select a format.

⑥ Click **Save**.

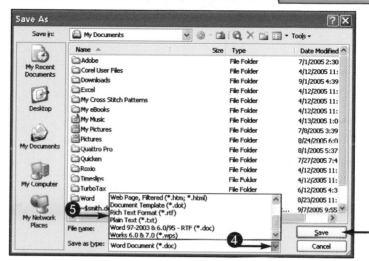

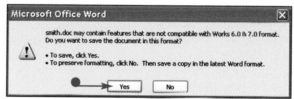

A dialog box may appear.

● You can click **Yes** or **OK** to save the document in the selected format.

Note: You may be prompted to install a converter to save the file in the selected format; click Yes or OK to install the converter.

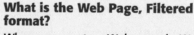

TIPS

What happens if I click the Save icon (⬜) on the Standard toolbar?

If you have not previously saved the document, the Save As dialog box appears; you can save a Word document or a file in a different format. If you previously saved the document, the Save As dialog box does not appear. Instead, Word simply saves changes you made since the last time you saved.

What is the Web Page, Filtered format?

When you create a Web page in Word, saving it using the other Web formats leaves Microsoft Word tags in the file so that you can continue to edit it as needed in Word. Use the Web Page, Filtered format if you are an experienced Web author who is concerned about the size of Web pages.

Set Options for Saving Documents

You can set a variety of options for saving documents, like whether Word creates a backup copy of your document and the location Word suggests when you save your documents.

Choose a save option ...

Set Options for Saving Documents

SET FILE SAVING OPTIONS

1 Click **Tools**.

2 Click **Options**.

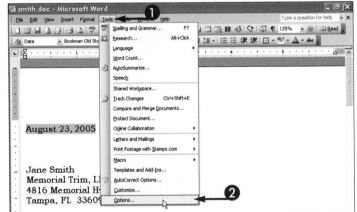

The Options dialog box appears.

3 Click the **Save** tab.

● You can click the **Allow fast saves** option (☐ changes to ☑) to speed up saving by saving changes only.

● You can click the **Save AutoRecovery info every** option (☐ changes to ☑) to save information to recover your document if your computer loses power.

4 Click **OK**.

Word saves your changes.

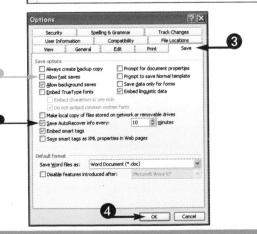

SET FILE SAVING LOCATIONS

① Complete steps **1** to **2** in the subsection "Set File Saving Options" on the previous page.

② Click the **File Locations** tab.

The File Locations tab appears.

③ Click a file type.

④ Click **Modify**.

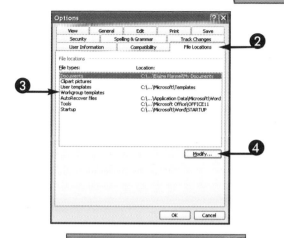

The Modify Location dialog box appears.

⑤ Click the **Look In** ⊡ to navigate to the folder where you want to save the selected file type.

⑥ Click **OK** to redisplay the Options dialog box.

⑦ Repeat steps **3** to **6** for each location you want to change.

⑧ Click **OK**.

Word saves your changes.

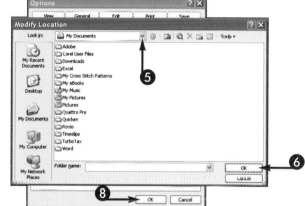

 TIPS

Why should I save fonts with my document?

You save fonts to enable others who use your document to also use the fonts that appear in the document. Typically, you must store a font on your computer to use it. However, when you embed fonts in a document, others who use your document can also use the document's fonts, even if they do not have the fonts on their computers.

What happens if I select the Always create backup copy option?

Each time you save your document, Word saves a copy of your document with a .wbk extension in the same folder as your document. You can click this option (☐ changes to ☑) in lieu of the **Allow fast saves** option, which saves time by storing changes only, to store permanent, complete copies of your document.

Open Documents

You can display documents you previously saved on-screen. When you open a document, you can make changes to it.

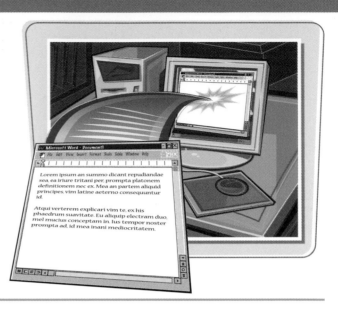

OPEN A WORD DOCUMENT

1 Click **File**.

2 Click **Open**.

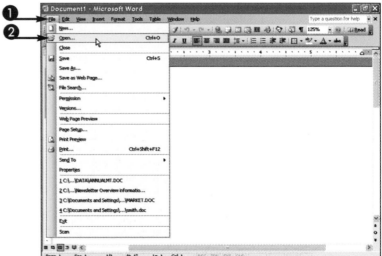

The Open dialog box appears.

3 Click the **Look in** ⬇ to navigate to the folder containing the document you want to open.

● You can double-click a folder to see the documents in it.

● You can click these buttons to navigate to common file locations.

④ Click the document you want to open.

⑤ Click **Open**.

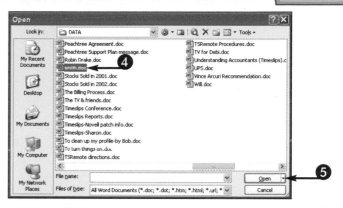

The document appears on-screen.

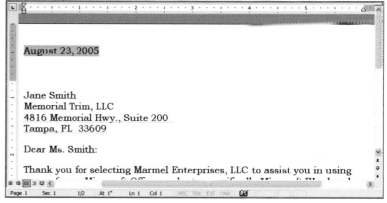

TIP

Are there other ways to open a document?

Yes. Recently used documents appear in the Getting Started task pane and at the bottom of the File menu. You also can click the **More** icon in the Getting Started task pane or the **Open** button ( ) on the Standard toolbar to display the Open dialog box shown in this section.

① Click **File**.

② Click a document to open it.

● Alternatively, you can click a document in the Getting Started task pane to open it.

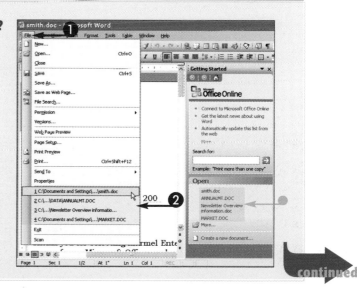

continued

You can open documents created by colleagues using several other word processing programs besides Word.

OPEN A DOCUMENT IN ANOTHER FORMAT

1. Click **File**.

2. Click **Open**.

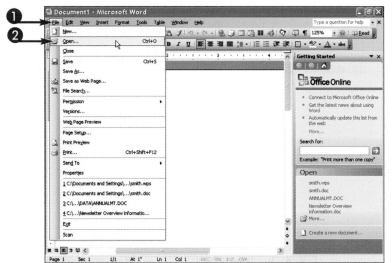

The Open dialog box appears.

3. Click the **Look in** ▾ to navigate to the file you want to open.

● You can double-click a folder to view the documents in it.

● You can click these buttons to navigate to common file locations.

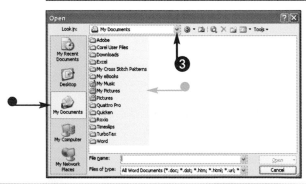

④ Click the **Files of type** ⊡ to select the type
of document you want to open.

⑤ Click the file you want to open.

⑥ Click **Open**.

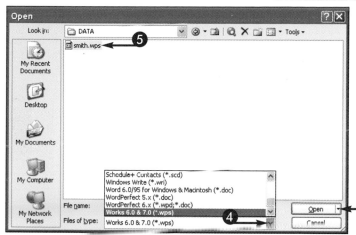

Note: You may be prompted to install a converter to open the file;
click **Yes** or **OK** to install the converter and open the file.

The Convert File dialog box appears.

⑦ Select the program that created the file.

⑧ Click **OK**.

Word opens the file.

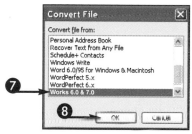

I set my Save options to create a backup copy. How do I open the backup copy?
Follow these steps:

❶ Follow steps **1** to **3** in this section.

❷ Click the **Files of type** ⊡ and click **All Files**.

❸ Click the arrow portion of ▦ ▾ and click ▦.

❹ Select the document.

In the Name column, the file name appears
as "Backup of" the original document.

In the Type column, "Microsoft Word Backup Document" appears.

❺ Click **Open**.

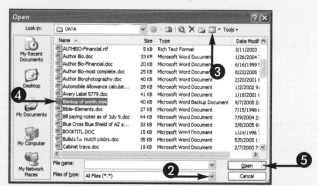

Although a new, blank document appears when Word opens, you do not need to close and reopen Word to start a new, blank document.

You can use a variety of templates — documents containing predefined settings that save you the effort of creating the settings yourself — as the foundation for your documents.

Start a New Document

❶ Click **File**.

❷ Click **New**.

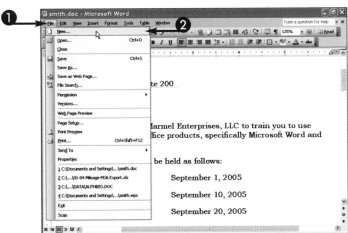

The New Document task pane appears.

❸ Click the **On my computer** link.

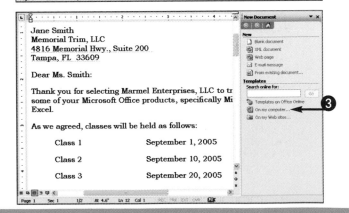

The Templates dialog box appears.

4 Click a tab to view the available templates in that category.

5 Click a template.

6 Click **OK**.

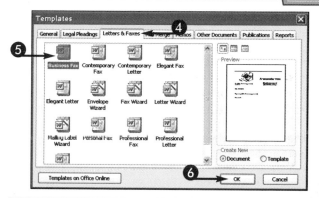

A new document appears on-screen.

You can edit this document any way you choose.

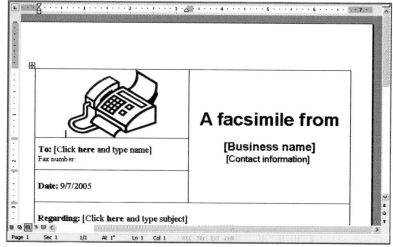

TIPS

How can I create a new document from scratch without closing and reopening Word?

You can click the **Blank Document** link in the New Document task pane, or you can click the **New** icon (⬜) on the Standard toolbar. You also can click the **Blank Document** icon (⬜) that appears on the General `Tab` of the Templates dialog box.

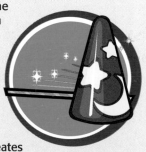

What happens if I select a wizard?

A wizard walks you through the process needed to complete a task. The Fax wizard, for example, asks you to identify the document you want to fax, the fax software you are using, the recipients and their fax phone numbers, the cover sheet you want to include with the fax, and the sender information. It then creates a cover sheet and helps you send the fax.

Switch Between Open Documents

If you have two or more documents open, you can switch between them using the Word menus or the Windows Taskbar.

If buttons representing each open document do not appear on the Windows Taskbar, you can set options to display them.

SWITCH USING THE WINDOW MENU

1 Click **Window**.

A list of all open documents appears at the bottom of the menu.

2 Click the document you want to view.

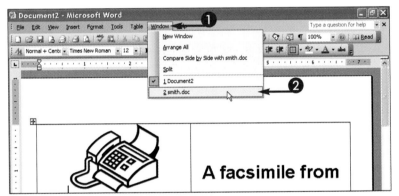

The selected document appears.

● You also can switch documents by clicking their Windows Taskbar buttons.

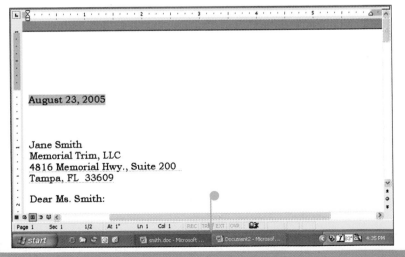

DISPLAY BUTTONS ON THE TASKBAR

1 Click **Tools**.

2 Click **Options**.

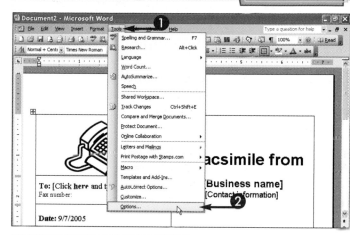

The Options dialog box appears.

3 Click the **View** tab.

4 Click the **Windows in Taskbar** option
(☐ changes to ☑).

5 Click **OK**.

Word saves your settings, and buttons for each
open document appear in the Windows Taskbar.

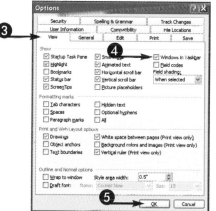

TIP

**I have several documents open and I want to switch to a
specific document, but I do not see buttons for all of the
open documents on the Windows Taskbar. What should I do?**

The buttons are there; the Windows Taskbar stacks them.

1 Click ▲▼ to view additional
buttons for open documents.

2 Place the mouse pointer on a button.

● A screen tip containing the
document's name appears.

3 Click a document to switch documents.

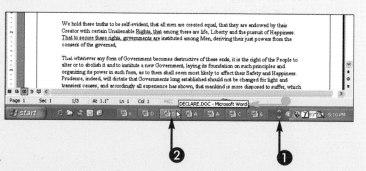

Compare Open Documents

You can view two open documents side by side on-screen to compare their similarities and differences.

Take the Challenge!

Compare Open Documents

1 Open the two documents you want to compare.

Note: See the section "Open Documents" for details on opening a document.

2 Click **Window**.

3 Click **Compare Side by Side with**.

Word displays the documents in two panes beside each other, along with the compare Side by Side toolbar.

4 Drag either document's scroll bar.

Word scrolls both documents simultaneously.

5 When you finish comparing the documents, click **Close Side by Side**.

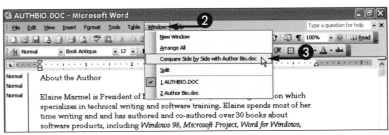

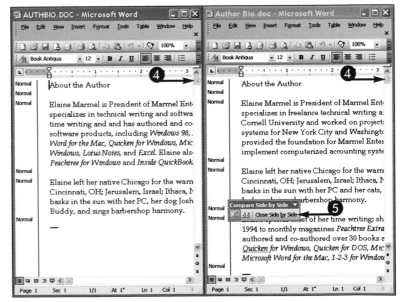

Close a Document

When you finish working with a document, you close it. If you made any changes that you did not save, Word will prompt you to save them before closing the document.

Close a Document

① Click **File**.

② Click **Close**.

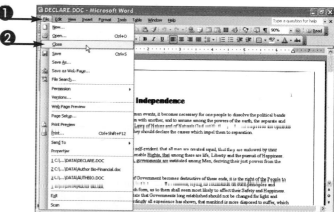

Word removes the document from your screen.

If you had other documents open, Word displays the last document you used; otherwise, you see a blank Word window.

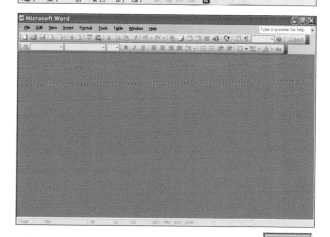

Search for a Document

You can use words or phrases to find documents. This feature is useful if you know the subject matter of a document but not the file name.

When you specify more than one word, Word displays documents that contain any — not all — of the words.

Find: "Four score and seven..."

❶ Click **File**.

❷ Click **File Search**.

The Basic File Search pane appears.

❸ Click here and type a word or phrase for which you want to search.

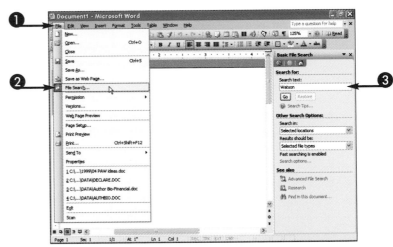

❹ Click ▼ to display the locations you want to include in the search.

● You can click a plus sign (⊞) beside a box to display additional folders.

❺ Click the box beside a location to include it in (☑), or remove it from (☐), the search.

❻ Repeat step **4** to close the list of locations.

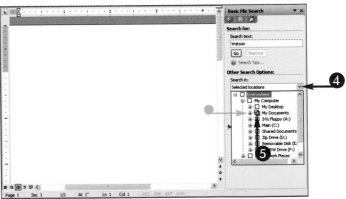

⑦ Click ⯆ to display the types of files to include in the search.

⑧ Click the box beside a file type (☐ changes to ☑) to include it in or remove it from the search.

⑨ Repeat step **7** to close the list of file types.

⑩ Click **Go** to search.

● The documents containing the word or phrase you specified appear.

You can open a document by clicking it.

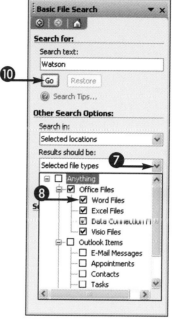

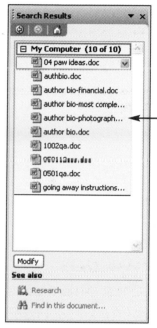

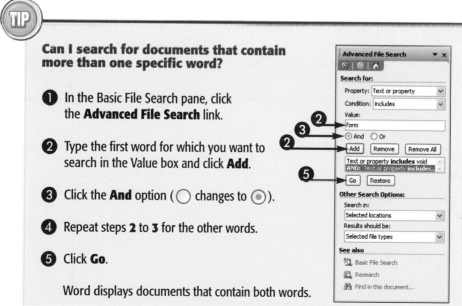

Can I search for documents that contain more than one specific word?

❶ In the Basic File Search pane, click the **Advanced File Search** link.

❷ Type the first word for which you want to search in the Value box and click **Add**.

❸ Click the **And** option (◯ changes to ◉).

❹ Repeat steps **2** to **3** for the other words.

❺ Click **Go**.

Word displays documents that contain both words.

Work with Protected Documents

You can limit the changes others can make to a document by protecting it with a password.

You can limit the styles available to format the document, the kinds of changes users can make, and the users who can make changes.

PROTECT A DOCUMENT

1 Click **Tools**.

2 Click **Protect Document**.

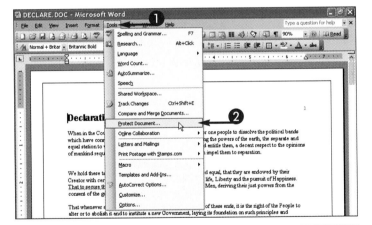

The Protect Document task pane appears.

3 Click here to limit document formatting to the styles you select (☐ changes to ☑).

4 Click the **Settings** link.

The Formatting Restrictions dialog box displays.

5 Click the styles you want available (☐ changes to ☑).

6 Click **OK** to redisplay the Protect Document pane.

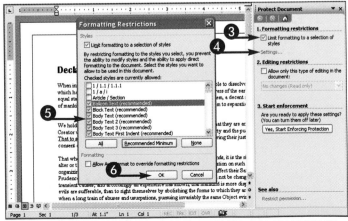

7️⃣ Click here to specify editing restrictions
(☐ changes to ☑).

8️⃣ Click here and select the type of editing to permit.

9️⃣ Select the parts of the document you want to make available for editing.

🔟 Click here to identify users allowed to edit the selected parts of the document (☐ changes to ☑).

⓫ Click **Yes, Start Enforcing Protection**.

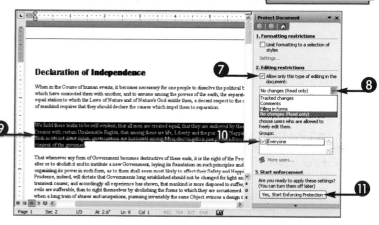

The Start Enforcing Protection dialog box appears.

⓬ Type a password.

⓭ Retype the password.

⓮ Click **OK**.

⓯ Click the **Save** icon 🖫.

Word protects the document and saves the protection.

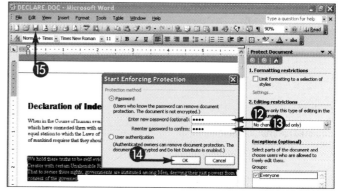

TIP

Can I protect a document so that only those with permission can open it?

1️⃣ Open the document you want to password-protect.

2️⃣ Follow steps **1** and **2** in this section, but click **Options** for step **2**.

3️⃣ Click the **Security** tab.

4️⃣ Type a password here.

5️⃣ Click **OK**.

Word prompts you to retype the password and click **OK**.

The next time you open the document, you must supply the password.

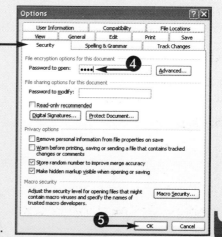

continued

Once you protect a document, Word permits only specified users to make the types of changes allowed by the protection.

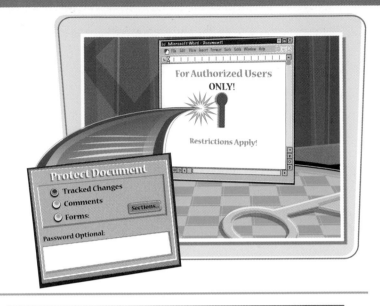

Work with Protected Documents (continued)

WORK IN A PROTECTED DOCUMENT

1 Open a protected document.

● Areas you can edit are highlighted.

2 Try to make a change in an area that is not highlighted.

● A message appears in the status bar, explaining that you cannot make the modification because that area of the document is protected.

3 Press **Ctrl** + **F1**.

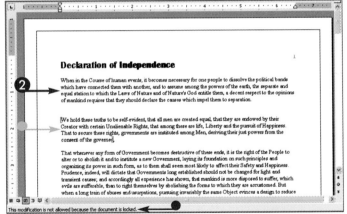

The Protect Document task pane appears.

Note: The appearance of the Protect Document task pane changes, depending on the type of protection you enabled.

4 Click **Find Next Region I Can Edit**.

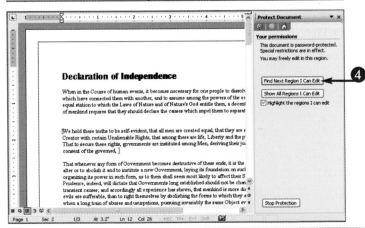

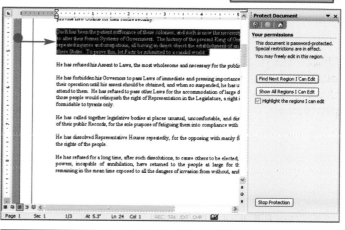

● Word selects and displays the next area available for editing.

You can edit the selected region.

❺ Repeat step **4** as necessary.

REMOVE PROTECTION

❶ In a protected document, display the Protect Document task pane.

Note: You can remove protection only if you know the document password.

Note: If the task pane is not visible, press **Ctrl** + **F1** .

❷ Click **Stop Protection**.

❸ In the Unprotect Document dialog box that appears, type the password.

❹ Click **OK**.

Word removes the protection.

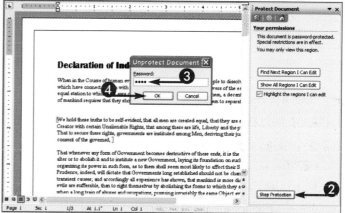

 TIPS

If I remove protection, do I lose all my protection settings?
No, Word retains the settings but does not enforce them. The protected areas become available for editing. The unprotected areas appear shaded in gray rather than yellow. You can make changes and then protect the document again by clicking **Yes, Start Enforcing Protection** in the Protect Document task pane and supplying a password.

What happens if I select Tracked Changes for the editing restrictions?
You do not see the **Find Next Region I Can Edit** button, the **Show All Regions I Can Edit** button, or the **Highlight the regions I can edit** option (☐ changes to ☑). Instead, a message appears explaining that the document is protected and that you can make changes but Word will track them.

CHAPTER

3

Edit Text

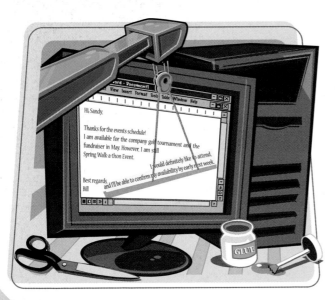

Once you know how to navigate around Word, it is time to work with the text that you type on a page. In this chapter, you learn editing techniques that you can use to change text in documents you create.

Insert Text

You can insert text into a document by adding to existing text or replacing existing text.

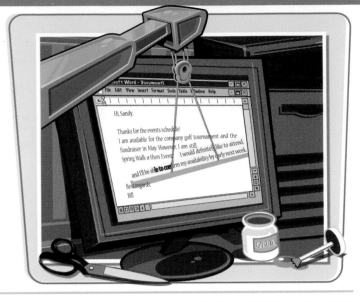

INSERT AND ADD TEXT

1 Click the location where you want to insert text.

The insertion point flashes where you clicked.

You can press ➡, ⬅, ⬆, or ⬇ to move the insertion point one character or line.

You can press **Ctrl** + ➡ or **Ctrl** + ⬅ to move the insertion point one word at a time to the right or left.

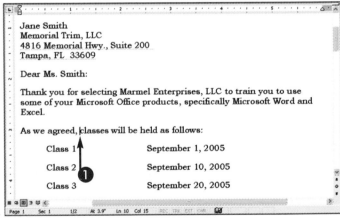

2 Type the text you want to insert.

Word inserts the text to the left of the insertion point, moving existing text to the right.

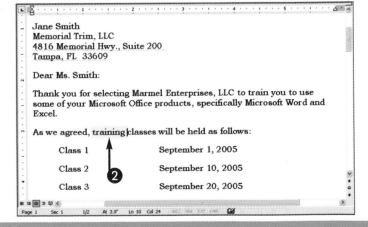

INSERT AND REPLACE TEXT

1. Press `Insert` on your keyboard.

● OVR appears on the status bar.

2. Click or press the arrow keys on your keyboard to position the insertion point where you want to insert text to replace the existing text.

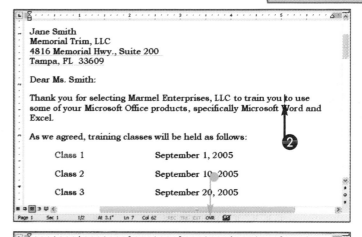

3. Type the text you want to insert.

Word inserts the text to the left of the insertion point, removing, character for character, any text that previously existed to the right of the insertion point.

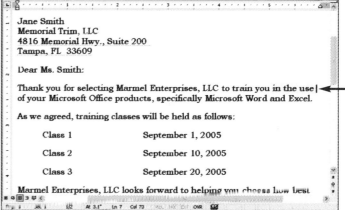

TIPS

How can I stop Word from replacing existing text when I insert new text?

Press `Insert` again. Each time you press `Insert`, Word toggles the Overtype feature on or off. Use the OVR indicator to help you identify when the Overtype feature is on or off. OVR is bold when the Overtype feature is on and dim when the feature is off.

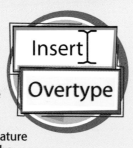

Is there a way I can use the keyboard to move the insertion point down by paragraphs?

Yes. Just as you can use `Ctrl` + `→` and `Ctrl` + `←` to move the insertion point to the right or left one word at a time, you can use `Ctrl` + `↓` and `Ctrl` + `↑` to move the insertion point down or up one paragraph at a time.

Delete Text

You can easily remove text from a document using either the Delete or Backspace keys on your keyboard.

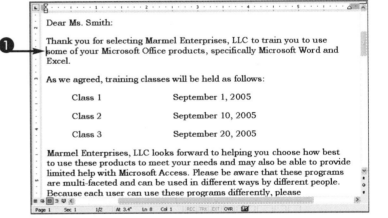

DELETE USING THE DELETE KEY

1 Click to the left of the location where you want to delete text.

The insertion point flashes where you clicked.

You can press ➡, ⬅, ⬆, or ⬇ to move the insertion point one character or line.

You can press Ctrl + ➡ or Ctrl + ⬅ to move the insertion point one word at a time to the right or left.

2 Press Delete on your keyboard.

● Word deletes the character immediately to the right of the insertion point.

You can hold Delete to repeatedly delete characters to the right of the insertion point.

You can press Ctrl + Delete to delete the word to the right of the insertion point.

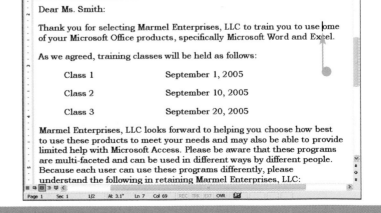

Dear Ms. Smith:

Thank you for selecting Marmel Enterprises, LLC to train you to use some of your Microsoft Office products, specifically Microsoft Word and Excel.

As we agreed, training classes will be held as follows:

Class 1	September 1, 2005
Class 2	September 10, 2005
Class 3	September 20, 2005

Marmel Enterprises, LLC looks forward to helping you choose how best to use these products to meet your needs and may also be able to provide limited help with Microsoft Access. Please be aware that these programs are multi-faceted and can be used in different ways by different people. Because each user can use these programs differently, please

Dear Ms. Smith:

Thank you for selecting Marmel Enterprises, LLC to train you to use ome of your Microsoft Office products, specifically Microsoft Word and Excel.

As we agreed, training classes will be held as follows:

Class 1	September 1, 2005
Class 2	September 10, 2005
Class 3	September 20, 2005

Marmel Enterprises, LLC looks forward to helping you choose how best to use these products to meet your needs and may also be able to provide limited help with Microsoft Access. Please be aware that these programs are multi-faceted and can be used in different ways by different people. Because each user can use these programs differently, please understand the following in retaining Marmel Enterprises, LLC:

DELETE USING THE BACKSPACE KEY

① Click to the right of the location where you want to delete text.

The insertion point flashes where you clicked.

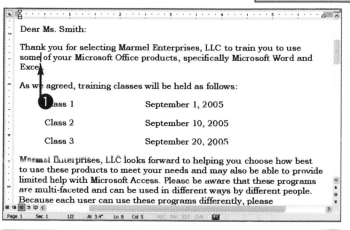

Dear Ms. Smith:

Thank you for selecting Marmel Enterprises, LLC to train you to use some of your Microsoft Office products, specifically Microsoft Word and Excel.

As we agreed, training classes will be held as follows:

Class 1   September 1, 2005

Class 2   September 10, 2005

Class 3   September 20, 2005

Marmel Enterprises, LLC looks forward to helping you choose how best to use these products to meet your needs and may also be able to provide limited help with Microsoft Access. Please be aware that these programs are multi-faceted and can be used in different ways by different people. Because each user can use these programs differently, please

② Press `Backspace` on your keyboard.

● Word deletes the character immediately to the left of the insertion point.

You can hold `Backspace` to repeatedly delete characters to the left of the insertion point.

You can press `Ctrl` + `Backspace` to delete the word to the left of the insertion point.

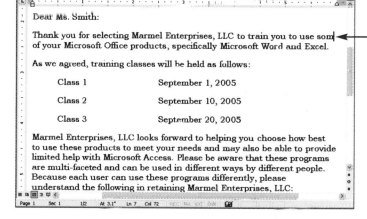

Dear Ms. Smith:

Thank you for selecting Marmel Enterprises, LLC to train you to use som of your Microsoft Office products, specifically Microsoft Word and Excel.

As we agreed, training classes will be held as follows:

Class 1   September 1, 2005

Class 2   September 10, 2005

Class 3   September 20, 2005

Marmel Enterprises, LLC looks forward to helping you choose how best to use these products to meet your needs and may also be able to provide limited help with Microsoft Access. Please be aware that these programs are multi-faceted and can be used in different ways by different people. Because each user can use these programs differently, please understand the following in retaining Marmel Enterprises, LLC:

TIPS

Do I have to delete a large block of text one character or one word at a time?

No. You can select the block of text and then press either `Delete` or `Backspace`; either key deletes selected text. For details on selecting text, see the section "Select Text," later in this chapter.

What should I do if I mistakenly delete text?

You should use the Undo feature in Word to restore the text you deleted. Click the **Undo** (⤺) on the Standard toolbar. For details on how this feature works, see the section "Undo Changes," later in this chapter.

Insert
Blank Lines

You can insert blank lines in your text to signify new paragraphs by inserting line breaks or paragraph marks. You use line breaks to start a new line without starting a new paragraph.

Word stores paragraph formatting in the paragraph mark shown in this section. When you start a new paragraph, you can change the new paragraph's formatting without affecting the preceding paragraph's formatting. For more information on styles, see Chapter 6.

Insert Blank Lines

START A NEW PARAGRAPH

1 Press Enter.

● Word inserts a paragraph mark.

2 Repeat step **1** for each blank line you want to insert.

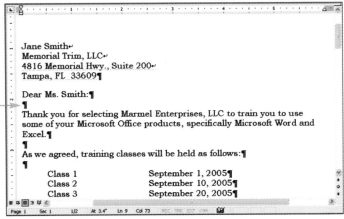

INSERT A LINE BREAK

1 Press Shift + Enter .

● Word inserts a line break.

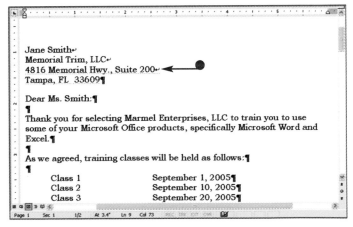

You can use the Undo feature to reverse actions you take while working in a document, such as deleting or formatting text.

The Undo feature is particularly useful if you mistakenly delete text; when you use the Undo feature, you can recover the text.

Undo Changes

1 Click the **Undo** icon (⤺).

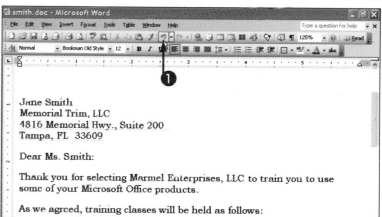

● Word reverses the affects of the last change you made.

You can repeatedly click ⤺ to reverse each action you have taken, from last to first.

You can press **Ctrl** + **Z** to reverse an action.

● If you decide not to reverse an action after clicking ⤺, click the **Redo** icon (↻ ▾).

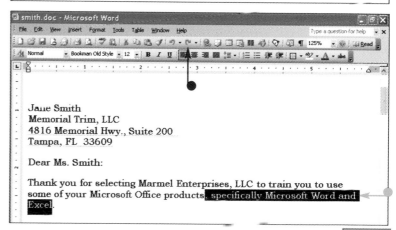

Select Text

Before performing many tasks in Word, you identify the existing text on which you want to work by selecting it. For example, you select existing text to underline it, align it, change its font size, or apply color to it.

SELECT A BLOCK OF TEXT

1 Place the mouse pointer (⬚) to the left of the first character you want to select.

2 Click and drag ⬚ to the right and down over the text you want to select.

● The selection appears highlighted in black.

To cancel a selection, you can press →, ←, ↑, or ↓, or click anywhere on-screen.

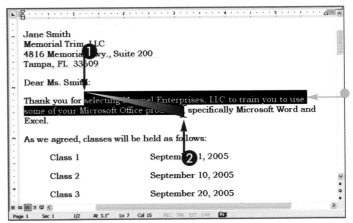

SELECT A WORD

1 Double-click the word you want to select.

Word selects the word.

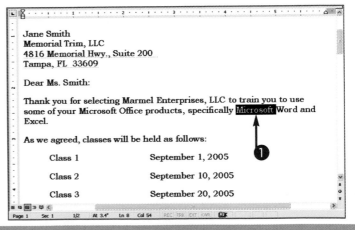

SELECT A SENTENCE

1 Press and hold **Ctrl**.

2 Click anywhere in the sentence you want to select.

Word selects the entire sentence.

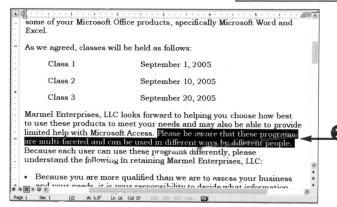

SELECT THE ENTIRE DOCUMENT

1 Press and hold **Ctrl**.

2 Press **A**.

● Word selects the entire document.

● You also can click **Edit** and then click **Select All** to select the entire document.

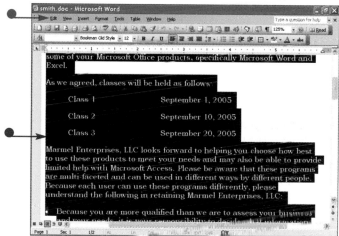

TIPS

Can I select text using the keyboard?

Yes. Press and hold **Shift** while pressing
←, →, ↑, or ↓.
You also can press
Shift + **Ctrl** to select,
for example, several words in
a row. If you press and hold
Shift + **Ctrl** while pressing →
five times you select five
consecutive words to the right
of the insertion point.

Can I select noncontiguous text?

Yes. You select the first
area using any of the
techniques described
in this section. Then,
press and hold **Ctrl**
as you select the
additional areas. Word
selects all areas, even
if text appears between
them.

Mark and Find Your Place

You can use the Bookmark feature to mark a location in a document so that you can easily return to it later.

You can also use bookmarks to store text; and Word uses bookmarks behind the scenes to operate some of its features.

MARK YOUR PLACE

1. Click the location you want to mark.

2. Click **Insert**.

3. Click **Bookmark**.

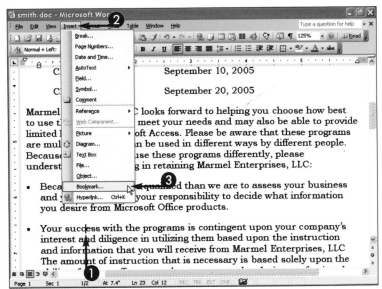

The Bookmark dialog box appears.

4. Type a name for the bookmark.

5. Click **Add**.

Word saves the bookmark and closes the Bookmark dialog box.

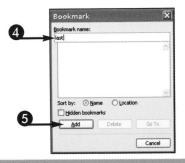

FIND YOUR PLACE

1 Press F5.

The Go To tab of the Find and Replace dialog box appears.

2 Click **Bookmark**.

3 Click here and select a bookmark.

4 Click **Go To**.

● Word moves the insertion point to the bookmark.

● A bookmark containing text surrounds the text with brackets ([ ]).

Note: If the bookmark contains text, Word moves the insertion point to the beginning of the bookmark.

5 Press Esc.

Word closes the Find and Replace dialog box.

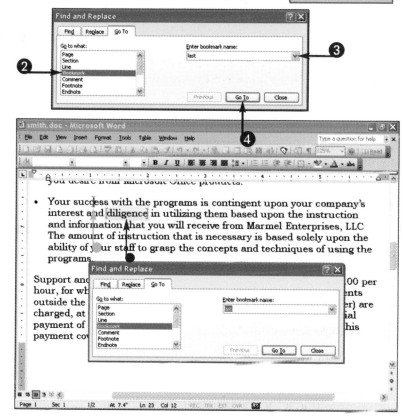

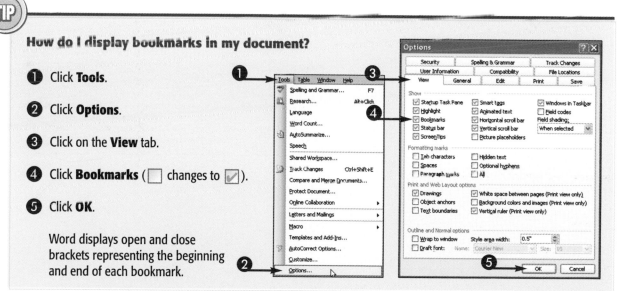

TIP

How do I display bookmarks in my document?

1 Click **Tools**.

2 Click **Options**.

3 Click on the **View** tab.

4 Click **Bookmarks** (☐ changes to ☑).

5 Click **OK**.

Word displays open and close brackets representing the beginning and end of each bookmark.

You can reposition text in your document by cutting and then pasting it. You also can repeat text by copying and then pasting it.

When you move text by cutting and pasting it, the text disappears from the original location and appears in a new one. When you copy and paste text, the text remains in the original location and also appears in a new one.

USING TOOLBAR BUTTONS

① Select the text you want to move or copy.

Note: To select text, see the section "Select Text."

② To move text, click either the **Cut** icon (◻) or the **Copy** icon (◻).

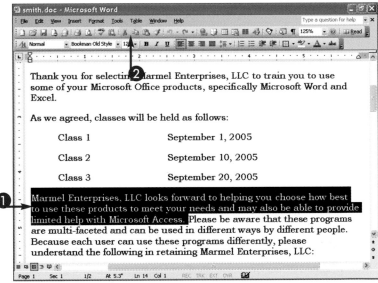

③ Click to place the insertion point at the location where you want the text to appear.

④ Click the **Paste** icon (◻).

● The text appears at the new location.

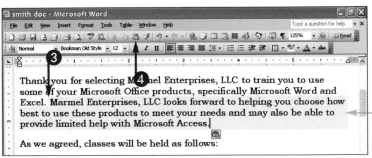

DRAGGING AND DROPPING

❶ Select the text you want to move or copy.

❷ Place the mouse pointer over the selected text
(I changes to ↖).

❸ To move text, drag the mouse (↖ changes to ↖); to
copy text, press and hold **Ctrl** and drag the mouse
(↖ changes to ↖).

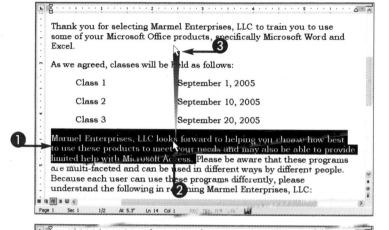

● The text appears at the new location.

TIPS

Is there a way I can move or copy text using menus?

Yes. You can select the text that you want to move or copy and then right-click it. A context menu appears; click **Cut** or **Copy**. Then, place the insertion point at the location where you want the text to appear and right-click again. From the context menu, click **Paste**. These three commands also appear on the **Edit** menu.

Is there a way I can move several selections at the same time?

Yes. You can click **Edit** and then click **Office Clipboard**. The Clipboard task pane appears, displaying up to the last 24 selections that you cut or copied. Cut each selection you want to move. Then, place the insertion point in the document where you want the text to appear. Click a selection in the Clipboard task pane to place it in the document.

Share Text Between Documents

When you cut, copy, and paste text, you are not limited to using the text in a single document. You can move or copy text from one document to another.

Any text that you cut disappears from its original location. Text that you copy continues to appear in its original location.

① Open the two documents you want to use to share text.

② Select the text you want to move or copy.

Note: For details on selecting text, see the section "Select Text."

③ Click 🔪 to move text or 📋 to copy text.

④ Switch to the other document by clicking its button in the Windows taskbar.

*Note: You also can switch documents by clicking **Window** and clicking the document's name at the bottom of the menu.*

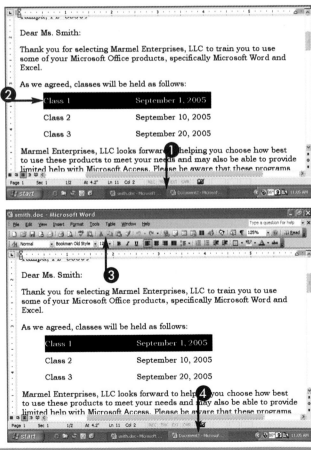

The other document appears.

5 Place the insertion point (I) at the location where the text you are moving or copying should appear.

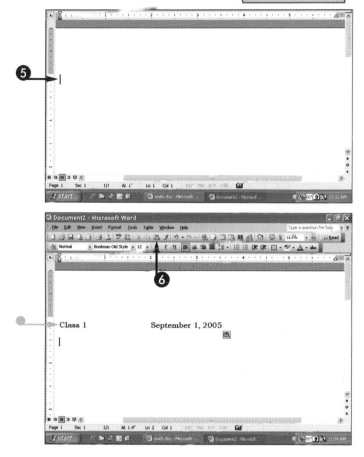

6 Click 📋.

● The text appears in the new location.

Class 1   September 1, 2005

TIPS

Why do I see 📋 when I paste?

Word displays the **Paste options** icon (📋) to give you the opportunity to determine how to handle the formatting of the selection you are pasting. Click 📋 if you want to keep the original formatting of the selection or to apply the formatting of the paragraph where the text appears after you have pasted it.

For text I paste, what format will Word use by default?

The default appearance of pasted text depends on whether you included the paragraph mark, which stores paragraph formatting information, in the selection you cut or copied. If you include the paragraph mark, Word pastes the formatting stored in the paragraph mark. When you exclude the paragraph mark, Word applies character styles or formatting but does not apply paragraph styles.

Switch
Document Views

You can view a document five different ways. The view you should use depends entirely on what you are doing at the time; select the view that best meets your needs. For more on the various views, see the section "Understanding the Document Views."

The button for the currently selected view appears in orange.

Switch Document Views

① To switch to a different view, click one of these buttons:

   ▤   Normal

   ▣   Web Layout

   ▤   Print Layout

   ▥   Outline

   ▥   Reading Layout

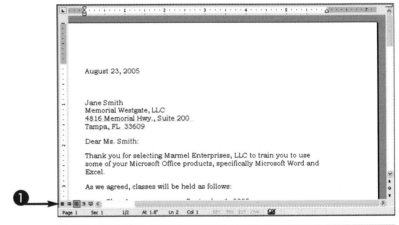

Word switches your document to the view you selected.

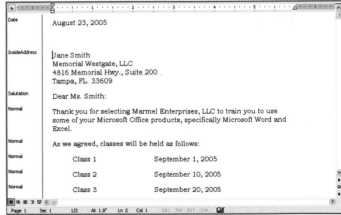

As mentioned in the section "Switch Document Views," you should select the view that best meets your needs. But, which view is right for you? The purpose of each view is described in this section.

To switch between views, see the section "Switch Document Views."

Normal View

Normal view is designed for editing and formatting; it does not display your document the way it will print. Instead, you can view elements such as the Style Area, but you cannot view the document's margins.

Web Layout View

Web Layout view is useful when you are designing a Web page or a document that you intend to view only on-screen.

Print Layout View

Print Layout view presents a "what you see is what you get" view of your document. In Print Layout view, you see elements of your document that affect the printed page, such as margins.

Outline View

Outline view helps you work with the organization of a document. Word indents text styled as headings based on the heading number; you can move or copy entire sections of a document by moving or copying the heading.

Reading Layout View

Reading Layout view is designed to minimize eye strain when you read a document on-screen. This view removes most toolbars. To return to another view, click the **Close** button (▦).

Work with the Document Map

You can use the Document Map view to navigate through a document that contains text styled in one of the Heading styles.

The Document Map pane is blank for documents that do not contain Heading styles. For more information on styles, see Chapter 6.

Work with the Document Map

1 In a document containing text styled with Heading styles, click **View**.

2 Click **Document Map**.

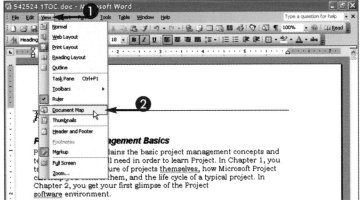

The Document Map pane appears.

● Each item in the Document Map pane represents a heading in your document; you can click any item to move the insertion point to that place in the document.

● You can click a minus sign (⊟) to hide subheadings.

Repeat steps **1** to **2** to hide the Document Map pane.

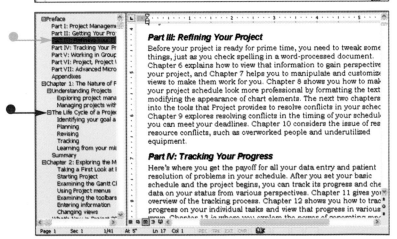

You can view thumbnails of each page in your document to get an impression of the visual appearance of each page.

You can also navigate to various pages using thumbnails. Thumbnails are not available in Web Layout view or when you are using the Document Map.

Using Thumbnails

① Click **View**.

② Click **Thumbnails**.

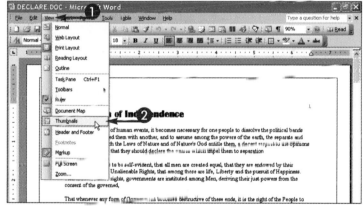

Word displays thumbnail views of each page in your document.

③ Click a thumbnail to view that page.

You can repeat steps **1** to **2** to hide the thumbnails.

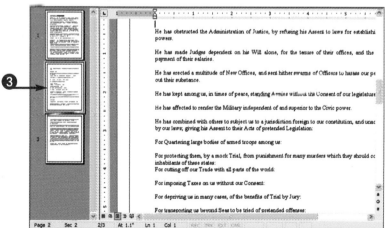

You can use the Zoom feature to enlarge or reduce the size of the text on-screen. Zooming in enlarges text. Zooming out reduces text, providing more of an overview of your document.

The available zoom settings change from view to view. See the section "Understanding the Document Views" for details on views.

Zoom In or Out

① Click ⌄ on the Zoom button (⌄).

② Click a zoom setting.

● You can click **Page Width** to fit the page, including margins, across the width of the screen or **Text Width** to fit text, excluding margins, across the width of the screen.

● You can click **Whole Page** or **Two Pages** to display one or two pages on-screen.

● The document appears on-screen using the new zoom setting.

Note: Text Width, Whole Page, and Two Pages are available only in Print Layout view.

Zoom settings do not affect the arrangement of text when you print the document.

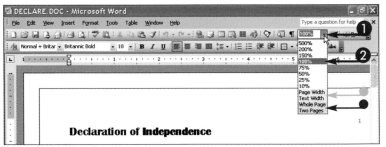

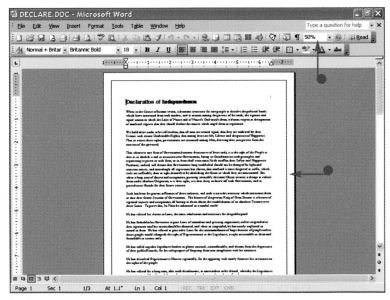

Toolbars contain buttons that help you select commands quickly. You can hide or display toolbars whenever you want.

The Standard and Formatting toolbars appear by default. Many other toolbars appear automatically when you start a particular task.

Hide or Display a Toolbar

1 Click **View**.

2 Click **Toolbars**.

A list of toolbars appears.

If a toolbar is currently active, it has a check mark (☑) beside its name.

3 Click the toolbar you want to display or hide.

You can skip steps **1** to **2** and right-click any displayed toolbar to view the list of toolbars.

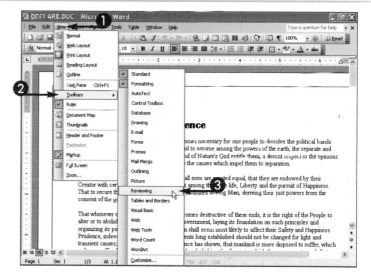

- Word displays or hides the selected toolbar.

- Word automatically parks some toolbars at the top of the screen while floating other ones.

  You can park a floating toolbar on any edge of the screen by dragging it.

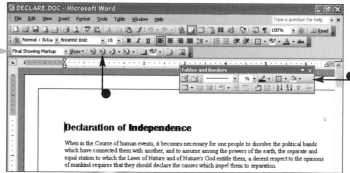

Insert a Symbol

Using the Symbol feature, you can insert characters into your documents that do not appear on your keyboard.

Insert a Symbol

① Click the location in the document where you want the symbol to appear.

② Click **Insert**.

③ Click **Symbol**.

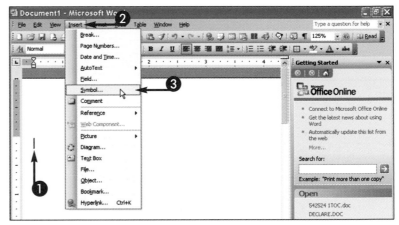

The Symbol dialog box appears.

④ Click here and select a font from which to select a symbol.

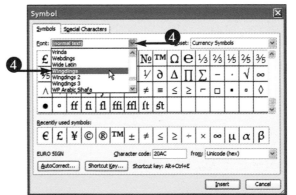

The available symbols change to match the font you selected.

⑤ Click a symbol.

⑥ Click **Insert**.

⑦ Click **Close** to close the Symbol dialog box.

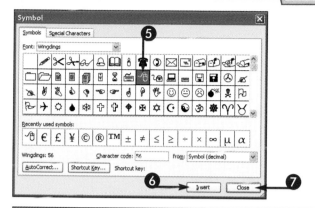

● The symbol appears in the document.

TIP

I use a particular symbol frequently; is there an easy way to insert it?

Yes. You assign a keyboard shortcut. Then, you can position the insertion point in the desired place and press the key combination to place the symbol.

① In the Symbol dialog box, shown in this section, click **Shortcut Key**.

② In the Customize Keyboard dialog box that appears, press **Alt** or **Ctrl** and any other key.

③ Make sure the combination is unassigned in the selected template.

④ Click **Assign**.

⑤ Click **Close** in the Customize Keyboard and Symbol dialog boxes.

The keyboard shortcut is assigned and ready to use.

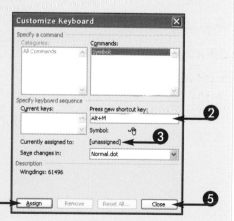

You can use smart tags to save time. Using Smart Tags, Word can open another program to get driving directions or a map to a location or schedule a meeting.

Word recognizes certain types of text and identifies them as smart tags by displaying a dotted purple line beneath them.

Using Smart Tags

① Move the mouse pointer (⌶) over a smart tag.

● The Smart Tag Actions icon (⬚) appears.

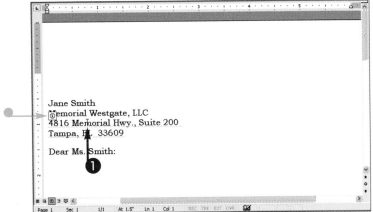

② Click ⬚ to display a list of actions you can take using the smart tag.

③ Click an action.

The program that performs the action you selected appears on-screen.

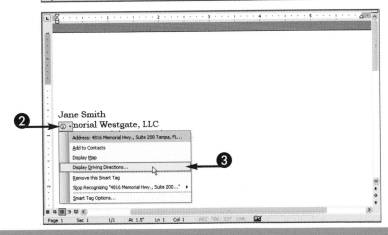

Set Smart
Tag Options

You can control the kinds of
information Word recognizes
and identifies as smart tags.

**You also can turn off smart tag
recognition entirely.**

❶ Click **Tools**.

❷ Click **AutoCorrect Options**.

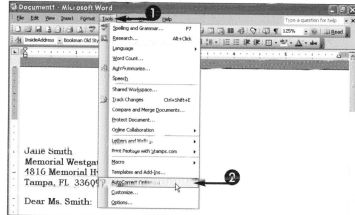

The AutoCorrect dialog box appears.

❸ Click the **Smart Tags** tab.

● You can click the **Label text with smart tags**
option (☑ changes to ☐) to turn off smart tag
recognition.

❹ Click the check box beside an item to turn smart
tag recognition on (☑) or off (☐).

❺ Click **OK**.

Word saves your changes.

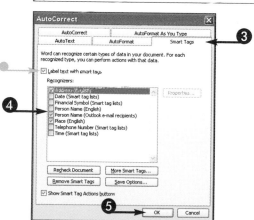

Translate Text

Using the Translation feature, you can translate a word from one language to another using language dictionaries installed on your computer.

If you are connected to the Internet, the Translation feature will search the dictionaries on your computer as well as online dictionaries.

Translate Text

1 Select the word you want to translate.

2 Click **Tools**.

3 Click **Language**.

4 Click **Translate**.

The Research task pane appears.

● The word you selected appears here.

● The current language translation pair appears here.

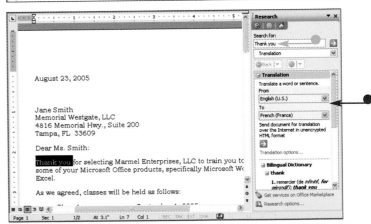

5 Click ☑ to display the languages available into which you can translate the selected word.

6 Click a language.

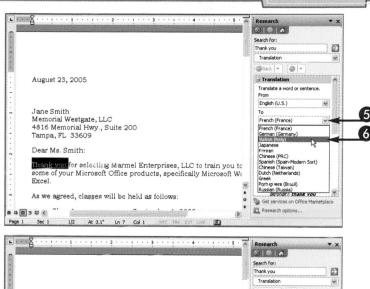

● The translation appears here.

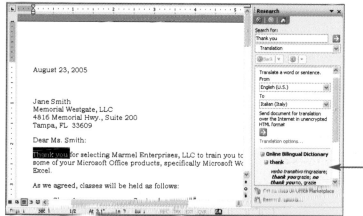

TIPS

No results were found when I tried to translate a word; what should I do?

Scroll down in the Research pane. You will find that Word suggests a variety of alternative spellings for the word you tried to translate. If none of them is correct, scroll further; you can try searching **All Reference Books** and **All Research Sites** by clicking their links.

Can the Translation feature translate my entire document?

Yes and no. While the feature is capable of fairly complex translations, it may not grasp the tone or meaning of your text. You can send the document over the Internet for translation, but be aware that Word sends documents as unencrypted HTML files. If security is an issue, do not choose this route; instead, consider hiring a professional translator.

Proofreading

Now that you have entered your text into your document, it is time to check your text. This chapter shows you how to handle proofreading tasks in Word.

Search for Text

Occasionally, you need to search for a word or phrase in a document. You may also need to change that word or phrase. Using Find and Replace, you can search and substitute as needed.

Search for Text

1 Click **Edit**.

2 Click **Find**.

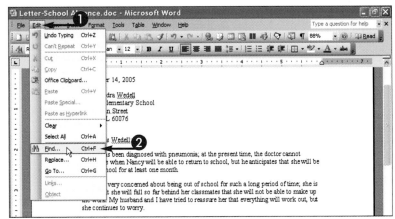

The Find and Replace window appears.

3 Type the word or phrase for which you want to search.

4 Click **Find Next**.

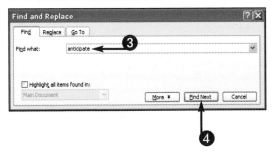

- Word highlights the first occurrence of the word or phrase.

- You can click **Find Next** again to find additional occurrences of the word or phrase.

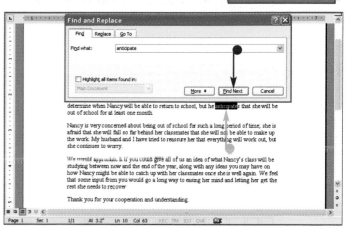

- When Word finds no more occurrences of the word or phrase, this dialog box appears.

⑤ Click **OK**.

⑥ Click **Cancel** to close the Find and Replace window.

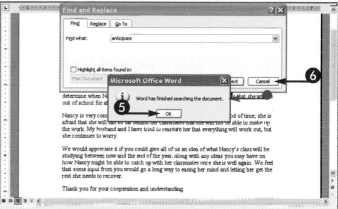

Does the location of the insertion point matter when I start searching?

No. Word searches from the location of the insertion point down through the end of the document and then, if necessary, continues searching from the beginning of the document. The search ends when Word reaches the location of the insertion point where the search began.

How can I make Word find "the" without finding "theology"?

You need to limit the search to whole words only. In the Find and Replace window, click **More**; the button name changes to **Less**, and the window expands to show additional options. Click the check box beside **Find whole words only** (☐ changes to ☑).

Often, you want to find a word or phrase because you need to substitute some other word or phrase for it.

You can substitute a word or phrase for all occurrences of the original word or phrase, or you can selectively substitute.

Substitute Text

① Click **Edit**.

② Click **Replace**.

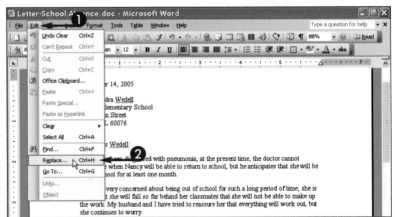

The Find and Replace window appears.

③ Type the word or phrase you want to replace here.

④ Type the word or phrase you want Word to substitute here.

⑤ Click **Find Next**.

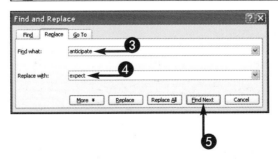

- Word highlights the first occurrence of the word or phrase that it finds.

- If you do not want to change the highlighted occurrence, you can click **Find Next** to ignore it.

6 Click **Replace**.

- To change all occurrences, you can click **Replace All**.

  Word replaces the original word or phrase with the word or phrase you specify as the substitute.

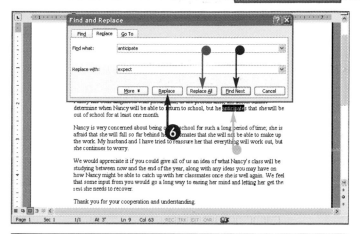

7 Repeat steps **5** to **6**, replacing or ignoring words or phrases as appropriate.

When Word finds no more occurrences of the word or phrase, a dialog box appears.

8 Click **OK**.

9 Click **Cancel** to close the Find and Replace window.

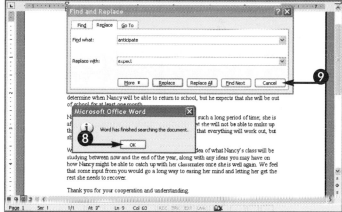

TIPS

Can I find italic text and change it to boldface text?

Follow steps **1** to **2** and click **More** to expand the window. Follow steps **3** to **4**, but, instead of typing text, click **Format** and then click **Font**. In the Font style list of the Font dialog box that appears, click **Italic** for step **3** and **Bold** for step **4**. Then complete steps **5** to **9**.

Can I search for and replace special characters such as tabs or paragraph marks?

Yes. Follow steps **1** to **2** and click **More** to expand the window. Then, follow steps **3** to **4**, but instead of typing text, click **Special** to display a menu of special characters. For step **3**, select the special character you want to find. For step **4**, select the special character you want to substitute. Then complete steps **5** to **9**.

Count Words in a Document

You can count the number of words in a document or in any portion of a document. This is particularly handy when you must limit the number of words in a section of a document. Make use of this feature when a work or school project requires a specific number of words.

COUNT WORDS OCCASIONALLY

1. Click **Tools**.

2. Click **Word Count**.

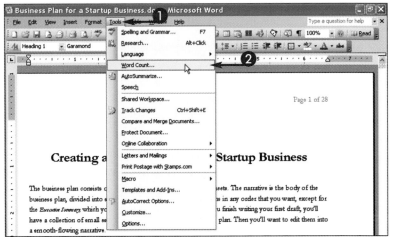

The Word Count dialog box appears.

● The Word Count dialog box reports the number of pages, words, characters with and without spaces, paragraphs, and lines in your document.

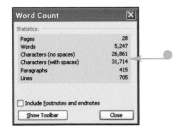

COUNT WORDS FREQUENTLY

1 Click **View**.

2 Click **Toolbars**.

3 Click **Word Count**.

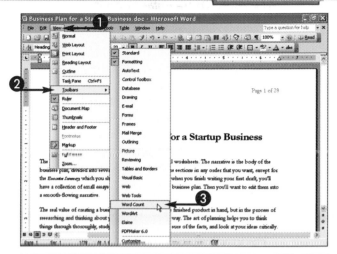

● The Word Count toolbar appears, displaying the total number of words in your document.

4 Add text to, or delete text from, your document.

5 Click **Recount**.

Word recalculates the number of words in the document and displays the updated count.

TIPS

How can I count something other than words when using the Word Count toolbar?

Click the ☑ beside the number of words displayed on the toolbar; from the list that appears, you can view the number of characters with and without spaces, lines, pages, and paragraphs. To continue counting something other than words, select the element you want to count.

Can I count the number of words in just one paragraph?

Yes. Select the text containing the words you want to count and then perform the steps to count them using either method described in this section. You can count any element, such as lines or paragraphs, by selecting them before counting.

Correct Mistakes Automatically

Using the AutoCorrect feature, Word automatically corrects hundreds of common typing and spelling mistakes as you work. You can also add your own set of mistakes and the corrections to the list Word references.

Correct Mistakes Automatically

1 Click **Tools**.

2 Click **AutoCorrect Options**.

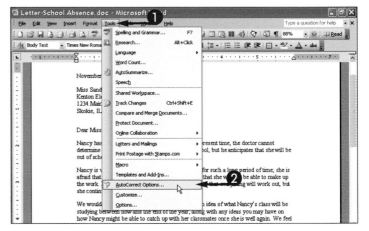

The AutoCorrect dialog box appears.

● The corrections Word already makes automatically appear in this area.

③ Click here and type the word you typically mistype or misspell.

④ Click here and type the correct version of the word.

⑤ Click **Add**.

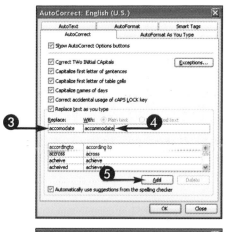

● Word adds the entry to the list of entries to automatically correct.

Repeat steps **3** to **5** for each automatic correction you want to add.

⑥ Click **OK** to close the AutoCorrect dialog box.

TIPS

How does the automatic correction work?

You do not need to do anything unusual – just type. If you mistype or misspell a word stored as an AutoCorrect entry, Word corrects the entry when you press Spacebar.

What should I do if Word automatically replaces an entry that I do not want replaced?

Position the insertion point at the beginning of the AutoCorrected word and click the **AutoCorrect Options** icon (B) that appears. From the list of choices displayed, click **Change back to**. To make Word permanently stop correcting an entry, follow steps **1** to **4**; when the stored AutoCorrect entry appears, click **Delete**.

Insert Frequently Used Text Automatically

Using the AutoText feature, you can store and then insert phrases you use frequently. The AutoText feature is particularly useful for phrases that take up more than one line, such as a name, title, and company name that appears at the bottom of a letter.

CREATE AN AUTOTEXT ENTRY

1. Type the text that you want to store, including all formatting that should appear each time you insert the entry.

2. Select the text you typed.

3. Click **Insert**.

4. Click **AutoText**.

5. Click **New**.

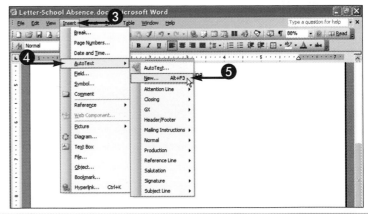

78

The Create AutoText dialog box appears.

6 Type a name for the entry.

Note: *If you avoid including vowels, Word will not confuse regular words with AutoText entries.*

7 Click **OK**.

INSERT AN AUTOTEXT ENTRY

1 Type the name you assigned to the entry.

● As you type, Word displays an AutoComplete tip.

2 Press `Enter`.

Word inserts the AutoText entry.

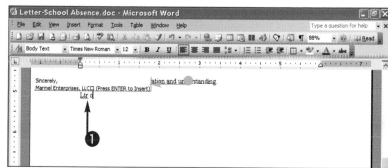

TIPS

What do I do if I cannot remember the name I assigned to an AutoText entry?

Word stores AutoText entries on the AutoText menu in categories. Click **Insert** and then click **AutoText**. On the side menu that appears, look for the Normal category; it contains most of the AutoText entries you create.

I do not see an AutoComplete tip when I type the name of the AutoText entry; what am I doing wrong?

You must make the name that you assign to your entry at least four characters long; if necessary, rename an entry by re-creating it. Then, make sure that AutoComplete is turned on. Click **Insert**, click **AutoText**, and then click **AutoText** again. In the AutoCorrect dialog box, click the **Show AutoComplete suggestions** box (☐ changes to ☑).

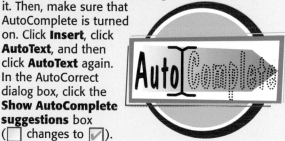

Using the Spelling and Grammar Checker, you can search for and correct all spelling and grammar mistakes in your document. On-screen, Word places a red squiggly underline beneath spelling errors and a green squiggly underline beneath grammar errors.

Word does not identify a misspelling when a word is correctly spelled but it is misused; for example, if you type "their" when it should be "there," Word does not flag it as a misspelling.

Check Spelling and Grammar

① Click **Tools**.

② Click **Spelling and Grammar**.

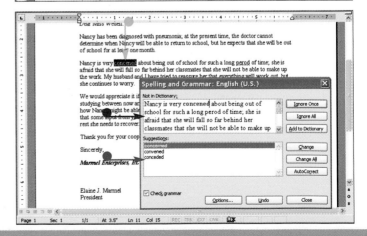

● Word selects the first spelling or grammar mistake and displays the Spelling and Grammar window.

Note: If your document contains no errors, this window does not appear.

● This area displays the spelling or grammar mistake.

● This area displays suggestions to correct the error.

③ Click the suggestion you want to use.

④ Click **Change**.

● You can click **Ignore Once**, **Ignore All**, or **Ignore Rule**, which appears for grammar mistakes, to leave the selected word or phrase unchanged.

Word selects the next spelling or grammar mistake.

⑤ Repeat steps **3** to **4** for each spelling or grammar mistake.

Word displays this dialog box when it finishes checking for spelling and grammar mistakes.

⑥ Click **OK**.

Can I correct spelling and grammar mistakes as I work instead of checking them all at once?

Yes. Each time you see a red or green squiggly underline, right-click the word or phrase. Word displays a menu of suggestions to correct the error.

When should I use the Add to Dictionary button?

Word identifies misspellings by comparing words in your document to its own dictionary; when a word you type does not appear in Word's dictionary, Word flags the word as misspelled. If the word is a term you use regularly, click **Add to Dictionary** so that Word stops flagging the word as a misspelling.

Disable Grammar and Spell Checking

If the red and green squiggly underlines that indicate grammatical and spelling errors annoy you, you can turn off automatic spelling and grammar checking.

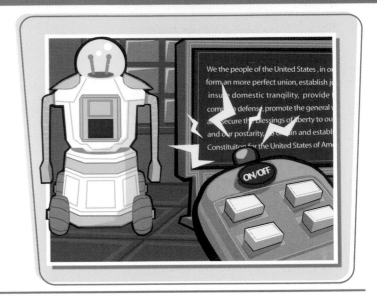

① Click **Tools**.

② Click **Options**.

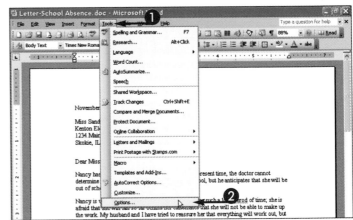

The Options dialog box appears.

③ Click the **Spelling & Grammar** tab.

④ Deselect the **Check spelling as you type** option (☑ changes to ☐) to disable automatic spell checking.

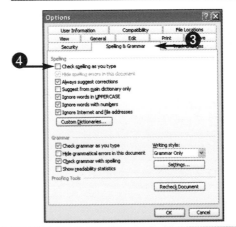

5 Deselect the **Check grammar as you type** option (☑ changes to ☐) to disable automatic grammar checking.

6 Click **OK**.

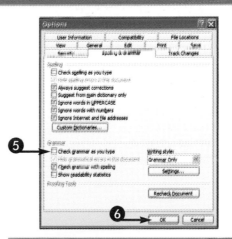

Word no longer identifies the spelling and grammar errors in your document.

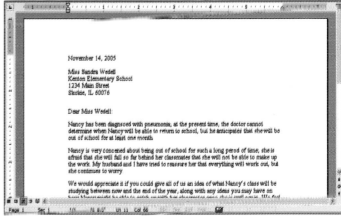

If I disable automatic spelling and grammar checking, is there a way to check spelling and grammar?

Yes. Use the procedure described in the section "Check Spelling and Grammar." When you follow the procedure in the section "Disable Grammar and Spell Checking," you are disabling only the portion of the feature where Word automatically identifies misspellings or grammar mistakes with squiggly red or green underlines.

What should I do if I change my mind and decide that I want to see the red and green squiggly lines?

Repeat the steps in this section, selecting the boxes you deselected previously (☐ changes to ☑).

Find a Synonym or Antonym with the Thesaurus

Using the Thesaurus, you can search for a more suitable word than the word you originally chose.

The thesaurus can help you find a synonym — a word with a similar meaning — for the word you originally chose, as well as an antonym — a word with an opposite meaning.

Find a Synonym or Antonym with the Thesaurus

① Click the word for which you want to find an opposite or substitute.

② Click **Tools**.

③ Click **Research**.

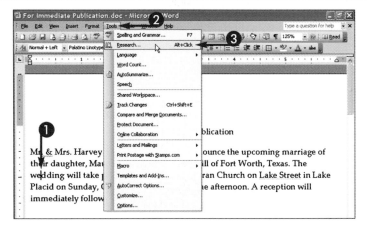

The Research task pane appears.

● The word you selected appears here.

④ Click ⊡ to display a list of resources you can use to search for information.

⑤ Click **Thesaurus**.

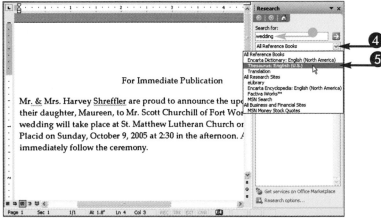

A list of words with similar meanings appears.

● Each bold word represents a part of speech – a noun, a verb, an adjective – with a similar meaning to the word you selected.

● Each word listed below a bold word is a synonym for the bold word.

● Antonyms are marked.

⑥ Point the mouse at the word you want to use in your document.

● ⌄ appears beside the word.

⑦ Click ⌄ to display a list of choices.

⑧ Click **Insert**.

Word replaces the word in your document with the one appearing in the Research task pane.

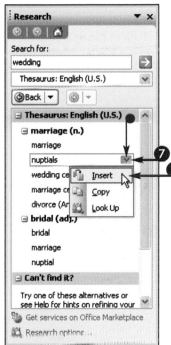

TIP

Is there a faster way I can display synonyms and antonyms?

❶ Click the word for which you want a synonym or antonym.

❷ Press Shift + F7 or right-click the word, and point to **Synonyms**.

❸ Click a choice to replace the word in your document.

Research
Information

Using the Research task pane, you can look up a word in the dictionary or search online resources for information on a variety of subjects using encyclopedias or online business resources.

Using online resources, you can search for essential business news and information to help you make better decisions faster, and you can get a stock quote.

Research Information

① Click a word in your document that you want to research.

② Click **Tools**.

③ Click **Research**.

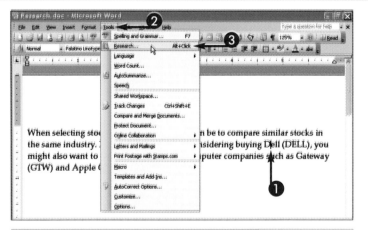

The Research task pane appears.

● The word you clicked in step **1** appears here.

④ Click 🔽 to display a list of resources available for research.

⑤ Click the resource you want to use.

Note: This example uses MSN Money Stock Quotes.

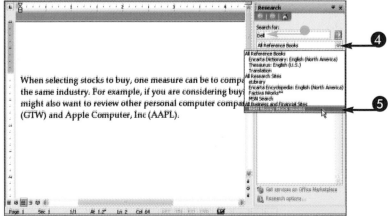

● Information from the research tool you selected appears in the Research task pane.

● Each of the research tools offers you a way to include the research in your document; the method depends on the tool, but in each case, you click  and then click **Insert**.

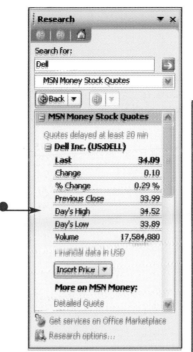

Can I find all of the research information for free?
No. If you must pay for the information, a link appears in the Research pane with a currency icon () beside it.

How can Factiva iWorks help me?
Factiva iWorks provides free Web search capabilities and is designed to provide access to content that helps employees make quicker, more informed business decisions. It is a streamlined version of Factiva.com, the fee-based search engine built into Microsoft Office 2003.

Add Comments to a Document

You can add comments to documents. You can use a comment to explain a statement, add a note of clarification, or remind you to take an action.

Comments are available in your document in Print Layout view or Web Layout view. You can view comments in the Comment pane in Normal view or Outline view.

ADD A COMMENT

① Click the **Reading Layout** icon (⬚), the **Web Layout** icon (⬚), or the **Print Layout** icon (⬚) to view your document.

② Select the text about which you want to comment.

③ Click **Insert**.

④ Click **Comment**.

● A comment balloon appears in the margin of the document.

● The comment balloon is attached to the text you selected, which is highlighted in the color of the balloon.

● Word displays the Reviewing toolbar.

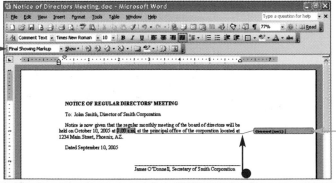

⑤ Type the text you want to store in the comment.

⑥ Click outside the comment balloon to save your comment.

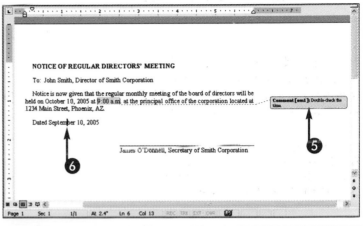

DELETE A COMMENT

① Click the comment balloon you want to delete.

② Click **Reject Change/Delete Comment** icon () on the Reviewing toolbar.

Word deletes the comment balloon and removes the highlighting from the associated text.

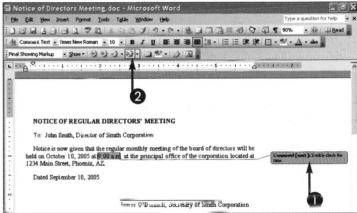

Can I insert a comment in Normal view or Outline view?

Yes. Follow steps **1** to **4**, selecting Normal view or Outline view in step **1**. When you complete step **4**, Word highlights the text you selected for comment and displays the insertion point in the Reviewing pane at the bottom of the document. Type your comment. To continue working, click in the document. To hide the Reviewing pane, click the **Reviewing pane** icon (▣).

What do the initials and numbers that appear immediately after the highlighted comment text tell me?

The initials represent the initials of the person who made the comment, and Word numbers each comment to help you distinguish between multiple comments by the same reviewer in the same document.

Track Document Changes During Review

Word can track the editing and formatting changes made to your document. This feature is particularly useful when more than one person works on the same document.

When Word tracks document revisions, it tracks the changes made and who made them so that you can easily identify who did what to a document.

① Click 📖 to display the document in Print Layout view.

② Click **Tools**.

③ Click **Track Changes**.

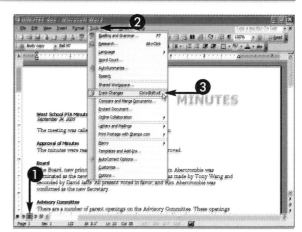

● The Reviewing toolbar appears.

● TRK appears in the status bar to indicate that Word is tracking changes.

④ Make changes to the document as needed.

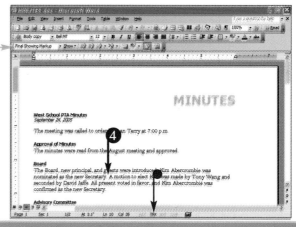

- A vertical bar appears in the left margin beside lines containing changes.

- Added text appears underlined and in a color other than black.

- Deleted text and formatting changes appear in comment balloons in the right margin of the document.

    Each reviewer's changes appear in a different color.

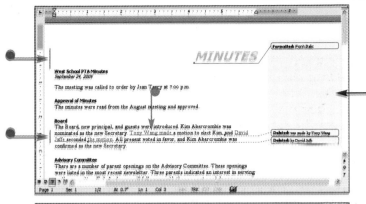

- You can view details about a change and who made it by moving the mouse pointer (ꆤ) over a change.

- You can stop tracking changes by repeating steps **2** to **3**, or you can click the **Track Changes** icon (📝).

Note: To review changes and accept or reject them, see the section "Review Tracked Changes."

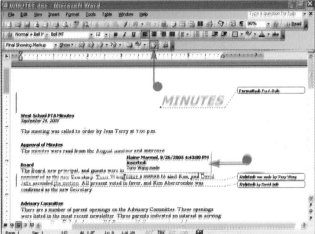

Can I print revisions?

Revisions will print as they appear on-screen based on the view when you print the document. You can, however, print a list of revisions from any view.

① Click **File**.

② Click **Print**.

③ Click here and select **List of markup**.

④ Click **OK**.

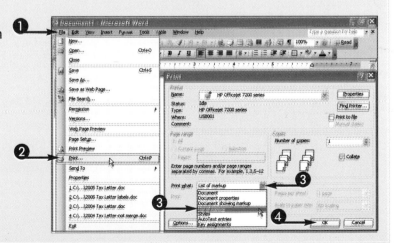

Review Tracked Changes

When you review a document containing tracked changes, you decide whether to accept or reject the changes. As you accept or reject changes, Word removes the revision marks.

1 Open a document in which changes were tracked.

2 Move ⊤ over any change to view details about it.

● Word displays the name of the person who made the change, the date and time of the change, and the details of the change.

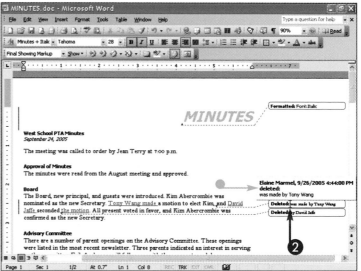

3 Press **Ctrl** + **Home** to place the insertion point at the beginning of the document.

4 Click the **Next** icon (⯈) to review the first change.

● Word highlights the change.

You can click the **Next** icon (⯈) again to leave a change unaffected.

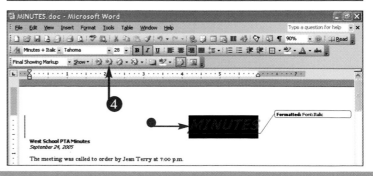

⑤ Click 🔲 to accept the change or 🔳 ▾ to reject it.

● Word accepts or rejects the change and removes the revision marks.

⑥ Repeat steps **4** to **5** to review all revisions; if you need to move backwards to a change you previously skipped, click the **Previous** icon (🔲)

When you have reviewed all changes, this dialog box appears.

⑦ Click **OK**.

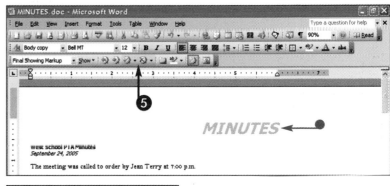

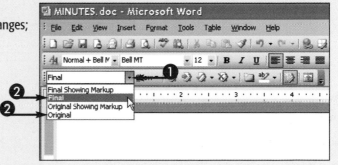

Is there a way I can work in the document without addressing the changes or viewing the tracking marks?

You can work viewing the original document before changes or viewing the edited document after changes; in either case, you can hide the revision marks.

① Click 🔽 on the Reviewing toolbar.

② Click **Final** to view the edited document without revision marks or click **Original** to view the document without revision marks, before any changes were made.

CHAPTER 5

Format Text

You can format text to emphasize it and make it easier for your reader to read. And, although the individual types of formatting are discussed separately, you can perform each of the tasks in this chapter on a single selection of text.

You can change the typeface that appears in your document by changing the font. Changing the font can help your reader better understand your document.

Use serif fonts – fonts with short lines stemming from the bottoms of the letters – to provide a line that helps the reader read. Use sans serif fonts – fonts without short lines stemming from the bottoms of the letters – for headlines.

Change the Font

1 Select the text that you want to change to a different font.

2 Click ☑ to display a list of the available fonts on your computer.

3 Click the font you want to use.

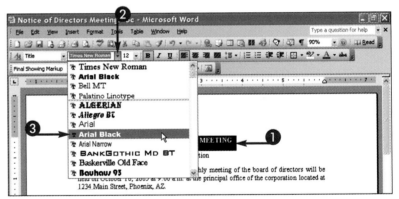

● Word assigns the font you selected to the text you selected.

4 Click anywhere outside the selection to continue working.

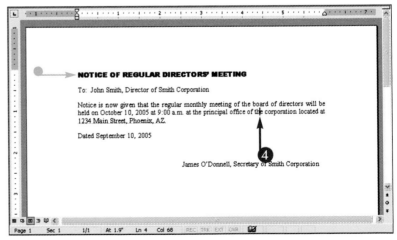

You can increase or decrease the size of the text in your document. Increase the size to make reading the text easier; decrease the size to fit more text on one page.

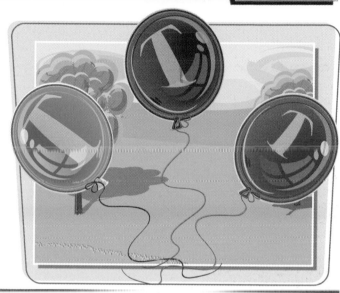

Change Text Size

1 Select the text that you want to assign a new size.

2 Click 🔽 to display a list of the possible sizes for the current font.

3 Click the size you want to use.

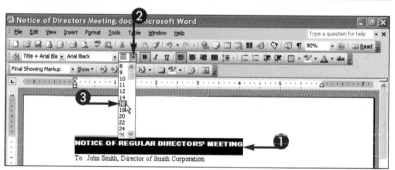

● Word changes the size of the selected text.

4 Click anywhere outside the selection to continue working.

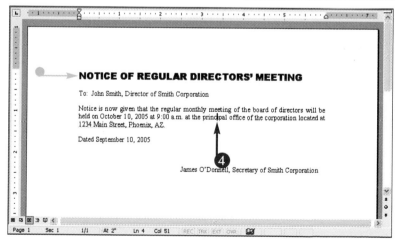

Emphasize Information with Bold, Italic, or Underline

You can apply italics, boldface, or underlining to text in your document to emphasize it.

1 Select the text that you want to emphasize.

2 Click the **Bold** icon (B), the **Italic** icon (I), or the **Underline** icon (U) on the Standard toolbar.

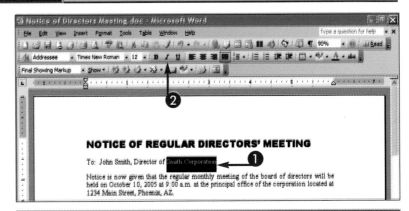

● Word applies the emphasis you selected.

3 Click anywhere outside the selection to continue working.

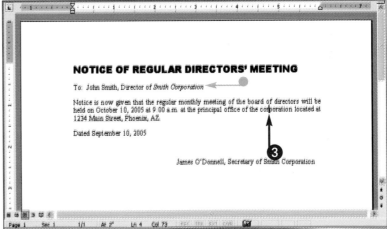

You can assign superscript or subscript notation to any text to make it appear above or below the regular line of text. Superscripting and subscripting are used often in mathematical and scientific equations.

Superscript or Subscript Text

① Type the text that you want to superscript or subscript.

② Select the text that you want to superscript or subscript.

③ Click **Format**.

④ Click **Font**.

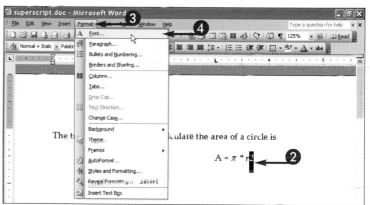

The Font dialog box appears.

⑤ Click either the **Superscript** or **Subscript** option (☐ changes to ☑).

Note: This example uses Superscript.

● You can apply any of these formatting options to selected text.

⑥ Click **OK**.

● The selected text appears superscripted or subscripted.

⑦ Click anywhere outside the selection to continue working.

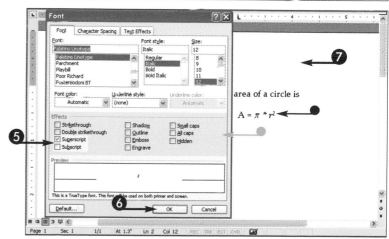

Change Text Case

You can change the case of selected text instead of retyping it with a new case applied.

Change Text Case

1. Select the text that you want to assign a new case.

2. Click **Format**.

3. Click **Change Case**.

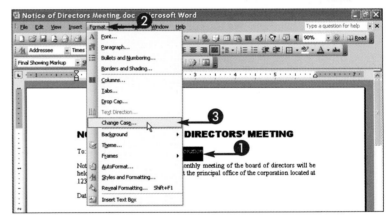

The Change Case dialog box appears.

4. Click the case you want to use.
   (○ changes to ⦿).

5. Click **OK**.

● The selected text appears in the new case.

6. Click anywhere outside the selection to continue working.

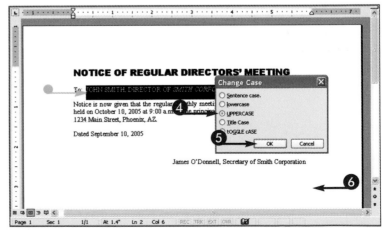

You can change the color of selected text to emphasize it. Color is effective when you view your document on-screen or print it using a color printer.

Change Text Color

1. Select the text that you want to change to a different color.

2. Click ☑ on the **Font Color** icon (🔺▾).

3. Click the color you want to assign to the selected text.

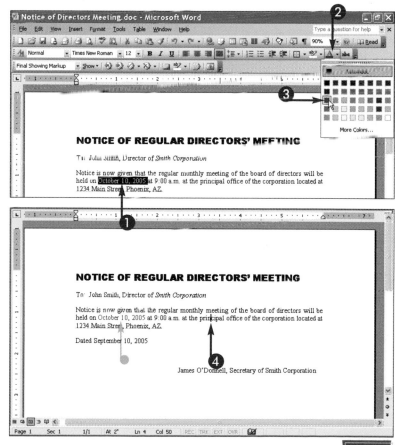

● Word assigns the color to the selected text.

4. Click anywhere outside the selection to continue working.

Apply Highlighting to Text

You can highlight text in a document using color to draw attention to it. Highlighting is effective when you view the document on-screen or when you print it using a color printer.

① Select the text that you want to highlight.

② Click ☑ on the **Highlight** icon (🔆▼).

③ Click the color you want to assign to the selected text.

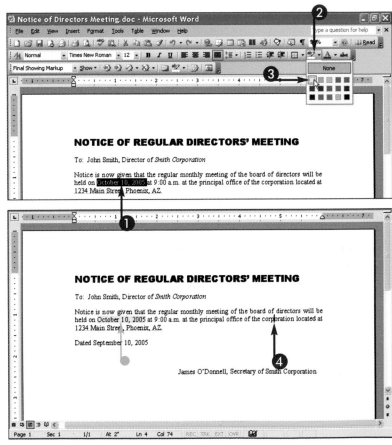

● Word highlights the selected text using the color you selected.

④ Click anywhere outside the selection to continue working.

To save time, you can copy formatting that you apply to text in one portion of your document to another portion of your document.

Copy Text Formatting

① Select the text containing the formatting that you want to copy.

② Click the **Format Painter** icon (🖌).

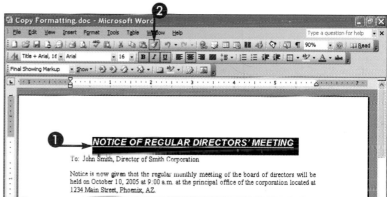

● The mouse pointer (🖑) appears as an icon (🖌) when you move it over your document.

③ Select the text to which you want to assign formatting.

● The newly selected text changes to the format used for the original selection.

④ Click anywhere outside the selection to continue working.

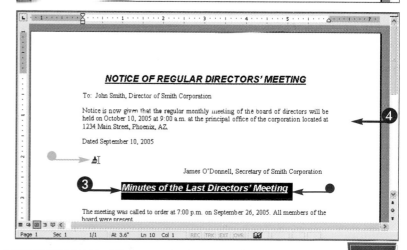

Remove Text Formatting

You can quickly and easily remove formatting that you have applied to text in your document.

Remove Text Formatting

1 Select the text from which you want to remove formatting.

2 Click **Edit**.

3 Click **Clear**.

4 Click **Formats**.

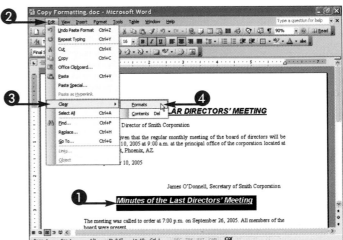

● Word removes all formatting from the selected text.

5 Click anywhere outside the selection to continue working.

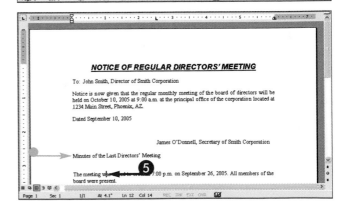

You can change the default font that Word uses for all new documents you create.

Changing the default font does not affect documents you have already created.

Set the Default Font for All New Documents

① Click **Format**.

② Click **Font**.

The Font dialog box appears.

③ On the **Font** tab, click to select the font, font style, and font size that you want to use for all new documents.

● A preview of the new settings appears here.

④ Click **Default**.

This dialog box appears, asking you to confirm the change.

⑤ Click **Yes**.

Word changes the default font.

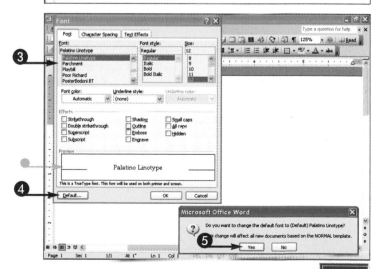

Format Paragraphs

Instead of formatting individual words in your document, you can apply changes to entire paragraphs to help certain sections of your text to stand out. You can apply formatting such as line spacing, bullets, or borders to the paragraphs in your document to enhance the appearance of the document.

You can change the amount of space Word places between the lines of text within a paragraph.

Word can measure line spacing in inches, but it is typically easiest to measure in points specified as pts. 12 pts equals approximately one line of space.

Set Line Spacing Within a Paragraph

① Select at least two lines of text to which you want to apply line spacing.

② Click the **Line Spacing** icon (⊡) on the Line Spacing button (⊟).

③ Click a number.

1 represents single spacing; **1.5** places 1/2 blank line between lines of text; **2** represents double spacing; **2.5** places 1-1/2 blank lines between lines of text; **3** represents triple spacing.

● Word applies the line spacing you specified to the selected text.

④ Click anywhere outside the selection to continue working.

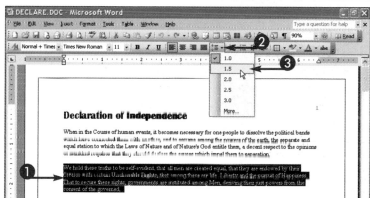

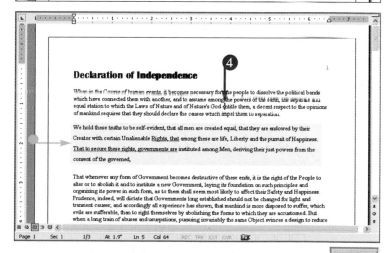

Set Line Spacing Between Paragraphs

You can change the amount of space Word places between paragraphs of text. For example, you can use this technique to set double-spacing between paragraphs while maintaining single spacing within each paragraph.

Set Line Spacing Between Paragraphs

① Select the paragraph or paragraphs for which you want to define spacing.

② Click **Format**.

③ Click **Paragraph**.

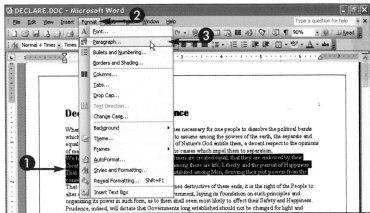

The Paragraph dialog box appears.

④ Click the spinner arrows (🔼) to increase or decrease the space.

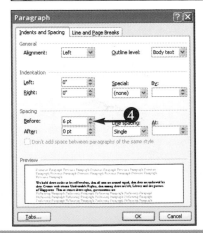

5 Click 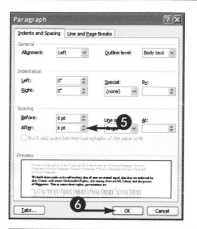 to increase or decrease the space after the selected paragraph.

6 Click **OK**.

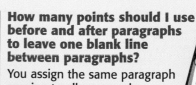

● Word applies the spacing before and after the selected paragraph.

7 Click anywhere outside the selection to continue working.

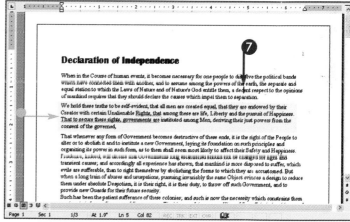

 TIPS

What does "pt" mean?

It is an abbreviation for "point," a measurement unit associated with vertical line spacing. A point is 1/72 of an inch. A 72-point line of text is approximately 1-inch high. Measure 1 inch of text vertically; in most cases, six lines of text fill 1 vertical inch of space. One line equals about 1/6 of an inch, and 1/6 of an inch equals 12 points of vertical line space.

How many points should I use before and after paragraphs to leave one blank line between paragraphs?

You assign the same paragraph spacing to all paragraphs. Assign 6 points before each paragraph and 6 points after each paragraph. The 6 points of space at the bottom of Paragraph 1 plus the 6 points of space at the top of Paragraph 2 equals 12 points, or one line space.

Create a Bulleted or Numbered List

When you present lists in your documents, you can use bullets or numbers to call attention to them.

Use numbers when the items in your list follow a particular order. Use bullets when the items in your list do not follow any particular order.

USING THE DIALOG BOX

① Select the text to which you want to assign bullets or numbers.

② Click **Format**.

③ Click **Bullets and Numbering**.

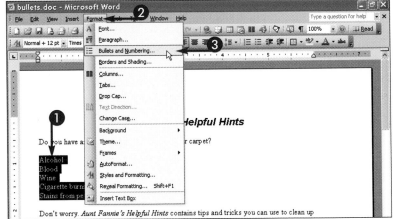

The Bullets and Numbering dialog box appears.

④ Click the tab for the type of list you want to create.

*Note: This example uses the **Bulleted** tab.*

⑤ Click the style of bullets or numbers you want to use.

⑥ Click **OK**.

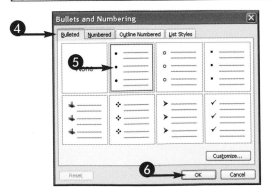

● Bullets or numbers appear at the left edge of each selected list item.

7 Click anywhere outside the selection to continue working.

To remove bullets or numbers, click the **Undo** icon (🔄), or repeat steps **1** to **6**, selecting **None** in step **5**.

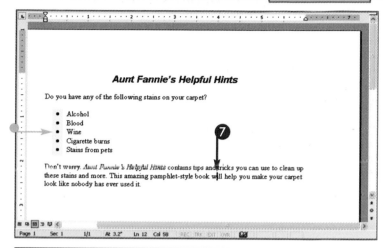

USING THE TOOLBAR

1 Select the text to which you want to assign bullets or numbers.

2 Click the **Numbering** icon (📋) or the **Bullets** icon (📋).

Word applies numbers or bullets to the selection.

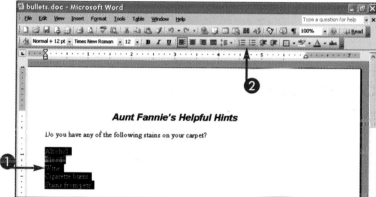

TIP

Can I create a bulleted or numbered list as I type?
Yes, you can do either one.

1 Type **1.** followed by a space to create a numbered list or * followed by a space to create a bulleted list.

2 Type the first list item.

3 Press Enter.

● Word automatically adds a bullet or number for the next list item.

4 Repeat steps **2** to **3** for each list item; to stop entering items in the list, press Enter twice.

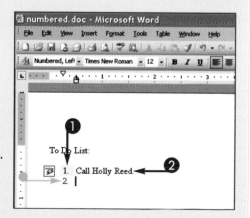

Indent Paragraphs

You can indent paragraphs in your document from the left and right margins. You also can indent only the first line of a paragraph or all lines *except* the first line of the paragraph.

① Select the text that you want to indent.

② Click **Format**.

③ Click **Paragraph**.

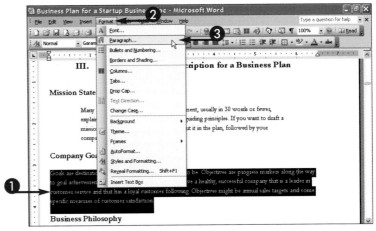

The Paragraph dialog box appears.

④ Click 🔽 to specify the number of inches to indent the left and right edge of the paragraph.

● The effects of your settings appear here.

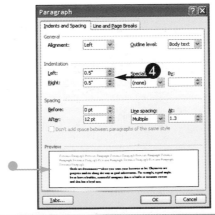

5 Click here and select an indenting option.

First line indents only the first line of the paragraph while **Hanging** indents all lines *except* the first line of the paragraph.

6 Click ⬍ to set the amount of the first line or hanging indent.

● The effects of your settings appear here.

7 Click **OK**.

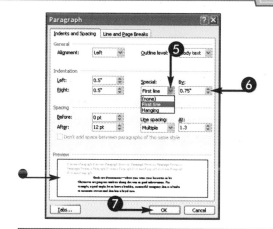

● Word applies your settings to the selected paragraph.

8 Click anywhere outside the selection to continue working.

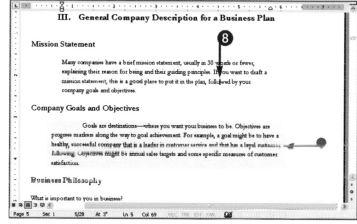

TIPS

Can I set paragraph indentations without using a dialog box?

Yes. You can use buttons in the Ruler. On the Ruler, drag the **Left Indent** icon (▢) to indent all lines from the left margin, drag the **Hanging Indent** icon (△) to create a hanging indent, or drag the **First Line Indent** icon (▽) to indent the first line only. On the right side of the ruler, drag ▢ to indent all lines from the right margin.

What do the Decrease Indent icon and the Increase Indent icon do?

The **Increase Indent** icon (▦) indents all lines from the left margin. The **Decrease Indent** icon (▦) decreases the indent of all lines from the left margin.

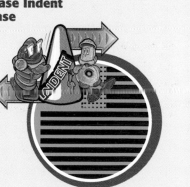

Set Tabs

You can use left, center, right, decimal, or bar tabs to line up columnar information. Using tabs ensures that information lines up properly within a column.

By default, Word places tabs every .5 inch across the page between the left and right margins.

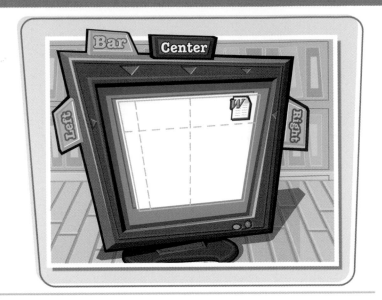

ADD A TAB

1 Click here until the type of tab you want to add appears:

- 🔳 Left tab
- 🔳 Center tab
- 🔳 Right tab
- 🔳 Decimal tab
- 🔳 Bar tab

2 Select the lines to which you want to add a tab.

3 Click the ruler where you want the tab to appear.

Word displays a tab at the location you clicked on each selected line.

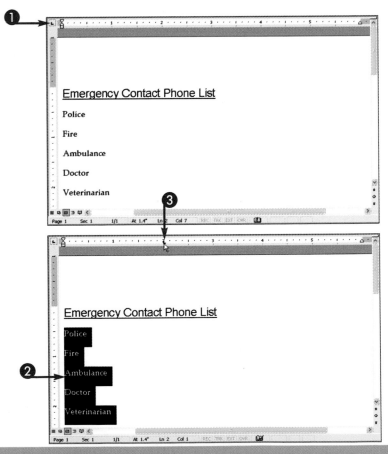

USING A TAB

1️⃣ Click to the left of the information you want to appear at the tab.

2️⃣ Press **Tab**.

3️⃣ Type your text.

⬤ The text appears at the tab.

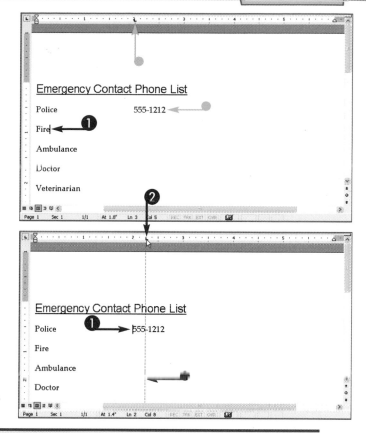

MOVE OR REMOVE A TAB

1️⃣ Click the line using the tab or select the lines of text affected by the tab.

2️⃣ Move a tab by dragging it left or right.

⬤ A vertical line marks its position as you drag.

You can delete a tab by dragging it off the ruler.

When you click and drag a tab, the text moves with the tab.

When you delete a tab, the text moves to the left on the line.

Can I set dot leader tabs?

1️⃣ Select the text containing the tab to which you want to add dot leaders.

2️⃣ Click **Format**.

3️⃣ Click **Tabs**.

4️⃣ In the Tabs dialog box, click the tab setting to which you want to add leaders.

5️⃣ Click a type of leader (◯ changes to ◉).

6️⃣ Click **OK**.

Word adds dots from the last character before the tab to the first character at the tab.

Add a Paragraph Border

You can add a border to a paragraph containing important information to draw attention to it.

① Select the text that you want to surround with a border.

② Click **Format**.

③ Click **Borders and Shading.**

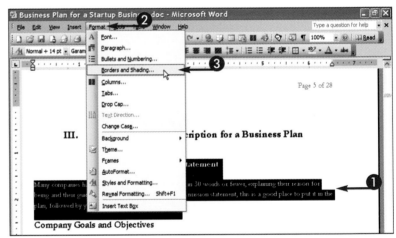

The Borders and Shading dialog box appears.

④ Click the **Borders** tab.

⑤ Click here to select a type of border.

Note: *This example uses* **Box**.

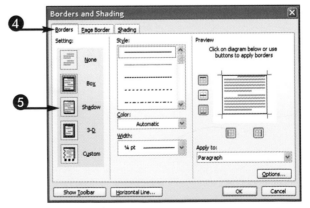

6 Click here to select the style for the border line.

7 Click here and select a color for the border line.

8 Click here and select a thickness for the border line.

● This area shows the results of the settings you select.

9 Click **OK**.

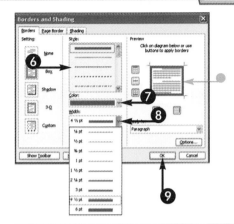

● The border appears around the selected text.

10 Click anywhere outside the selection to continue working.

● You can remove the border by clicking , or by repeating steps **1** to **5**, selecting **None** in step **5**, and then clicking **OK**.

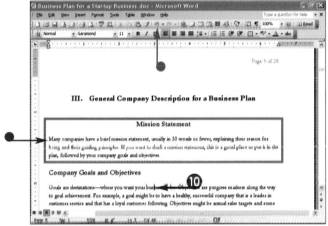

TIP

Is there a faster way I can add a border to a paragraph?

If you are willing to forego setting the color, style, and thickness of the border, you can use the **Border** icon ( ).

1 Select the text that you want to surround with a border.

2 Click   on   to display the types of borders.

3 Click a border type.

Word applies the border.

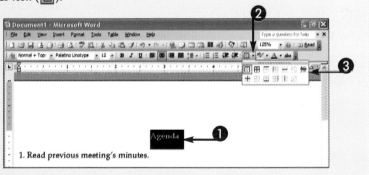

Add Paragraph Shading

Shading is another technique you can use to draw your reader's attention. Shading appears when you print your document; if you do not use a color printer, make sure you select a shade of gray for your shading.

① Select the text that you want to shade.

② Click **Format**.

③ Click **Borders and Shading**.

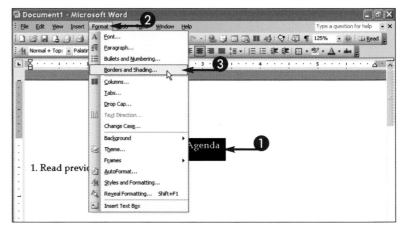

The Borders and Shading dialog box appears.

④ Click the **Shading** tab.

● The colors you can select for shading appear here.

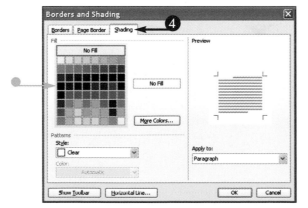

⑤ Click the color you want to use to shade the selected text.

● This area shows you how the shading will look.

⑥ Click **OK**.

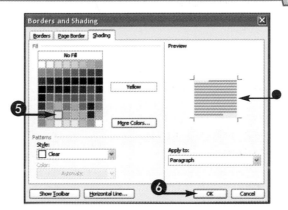

● Word applies the shading you chose to the selected text.

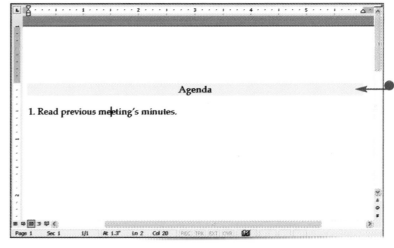

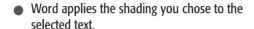

Agenda

1. Read previous meeting's minutes.

TIPS

How can I remove paragraph shading?
You can remove shading by clicking 🔄 or by repeating steps **1** to **5**, clicking **No Fill** in step **5**, and then clicking **OK**.

Can I apply a pattern along with shading?
Yes, you can, but exercise caution. A pattern alone can make the selected text difficult to read; adding both a pattern and a shading color may make the text completely illegible.

Check for Formatting Inconsistencies

You can have Word mark, with wavy blue underlines, text you have formatted inconsistently in your document. This feature is useful when you want to make sure that you have applied direct formatting, such as italics, consistently or that you have used styles whenever possible.

For each formatting inconsistency, Word suggests a way that you can make the formatting consistent and give your document a more professional-looking appearance.

DISPLAY FORMAT INCONSISTENCIES

1️⃣ Click **Tools**.

2️⃣ Click **Options**.

The Options dialog box appears.

3️⃣ Click the **Edit** tab.

4️⃣ Click **Mark formatting inconsistencies** (☐ changes to ☑).

5️⃣ Click **OK**.

Word saves your settings.

Formatting inconsistencies appear with wavy blue underlines.

CORRECT FORMATTING INCONSISTENCIES

1 Right-click a formatting inconsistency to display a menu.

2 To correct the inconsistency, click the first option on the menu.

● You can ignore this inconsistency by clicking **Ignore Once**.

● You can ignore all occurrences of this inconsistency by clicking **Ignore Rule**.

● Word selects the inconsistency, corrects or ignores it, and removes the wavy blue underline.

3 Click anywhere outside the selection to continue working.

4 Repeat steps **1** to **2** for each inconsistency.

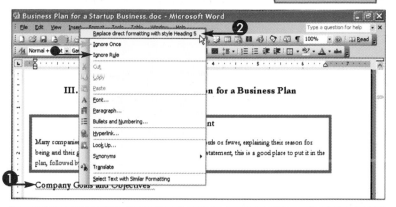

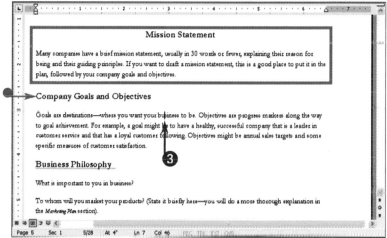

TIPS

What kinds of formatting inconsistencies does Word check for?

Word looks for occurrences of similar, but not identical, formatting that you applied directly to text or lists. Word also looks for occurrences of formatting you applied directly to text that matches styles you applied elsewhere in your document.

I do not want Word to check for formatting inconsistencies any longer. How do I turn off this feature?

Repeat steps **1** to **5** in the subsection "Display Format Inconsistencies." Deselect the **Mark formatting inconsistencies** option in step **4** (☑ changes to ☐). When you click **OK** in step **5**, Word disables the feature.

Review and Change Formatting

You can review the formatting associated with text in your document to see the details of exactly what formatting is applied to the text.

1 Select the text containing the formatting you want to review.

2 Click **Format**.

3 Click **Reveal Formatting**.

The Reveal Formatting task pane appears.

● A portion of the selected text appears here.

● Formatting details for the selected text appear here.

Note: You can click a plus sign (⊞) beside a bold heading in the Reveal Formatting pane to display links.

4 Click the link for the type of change you want to make.

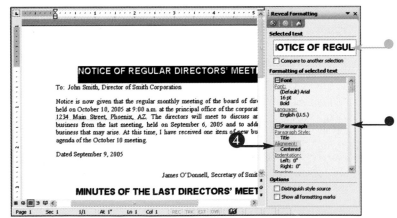

In this example, the Indents and Spacing tab of the Paragraph dialog box appears.

5 Select the options you want to change.

6 Click **OK**.

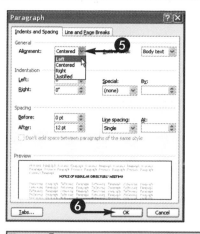

● Word applies the formatting changes.

● The information in the Reveal Formatting task pane updates.

7 Click anywhere to continue working.

● You can click the **Close** icon (⊠) to close the Reveal Formatting task pane.

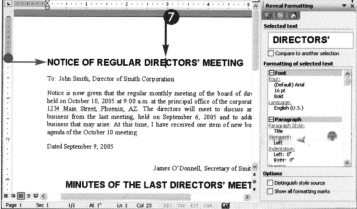

TIPS

What happens if I click the Distinguish style source option below the Reveal Formatting task pane?

When you click this option (☐ changes to ☑), Word changes the appearance of the Reveal Formatting task pane to include the names of any styles used in your document. For more information on using styles, see the section "Apply Formatting Using Styles."

Suppose that I want the font to be 18 points instead of 16 points; must I change each affected selection individually?

No. You can select one block of text and move the mouse over the Selected Text area. Click ⊡ that appears and click **Select All Text With Similar Formatting**. Make the font change, and Word changes all selected text. Also see the section "Apply Formatting Using Styles."

Compare Formatting

You can compare the formatting of one selection to another and have Word update one of the selections so that it matches the other. This feature is useful for ensuring that you apply consistent manual formatting to multiple selections.

① Select the text containing the formatting that you want to compare.

② Click **Format**.

③ Click **Reveal Formatting**.

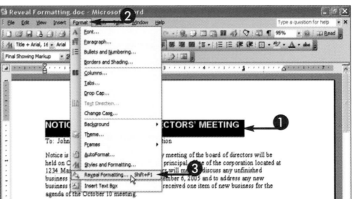

The Reveal Formatting pane appears.

④ Click the **Compare to another selection** option (☐ changes to ☑).

⑤ Select the text that you want to compare to the text you selected in step **1**.

● The two selections appear here.

● Formatting differences between the selections appear here.

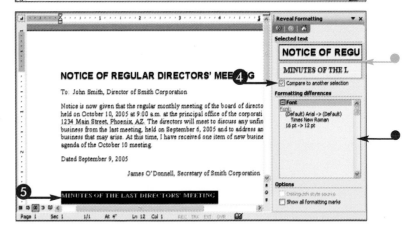

6 To match the formatting of the second selection to the formatting of the first selection, move the mouse pointer (⬐) over the area showing the second selection.

A ⬇ appears.

7 Click ⬇ to display a list of options.

8 Click **Apply Formatting of Original Selection**.

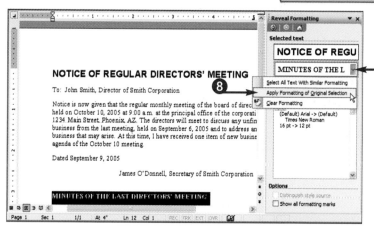

● Word applies the formatting of the first selection to the second selection.

9 Click anywhere to continue working.

● When the formatting of both selections matches, Word displays **No Formatting differences** here.

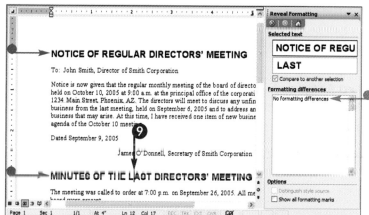

TIPS

What kind of formatting differences does Word identify in the Reveal Formatting task pane?

For any two selections, Word identifies differences in font, paragraph style, alignment, outline level, spacing before and after the paragraphs, line and page breaks, and bullets and numbering. You can make changes to any of these formatting differences by following the steps in the section "Review and Change Formatting."

What happens if I click the Show all formatting marks option below the Reveal Formatting task pane?

When you click this option (☐ changes to ☑), Word displays formatting marks in your document that represent tabs, spaces, paragraphs, line breaks, and so on.

Apply Formatting Using Styles

You can quickly apply formatting and maintain formatting consistency by using styles to format text. Styles are predefined sets of formatting that can include font, paragraph, list, and border and shading information.

① Select the text to which you want to apply formatting.

② Click the **Styles and Formatting** icon (⊞).

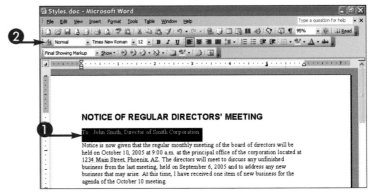

Word displays the Styles and Formatting task pane.

● The style for the selected text appears here.

● Available formatting styles appear here.

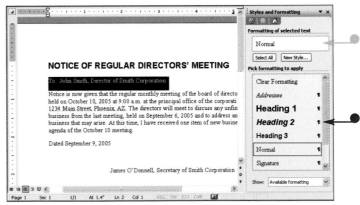

● You can point � at a formatting choice to display the details of the formatting.

❸ Based on the sample's appearance, click the style you want to apply to the selection.

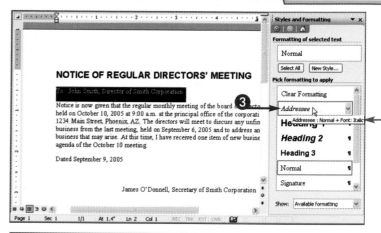

● Word applies the style to the selected text.

❹ Click anywhere outside the selection to continue working.

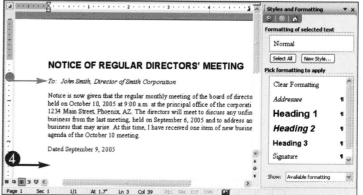

Is there an easy way to see, at a glance, the style assigned to each line or paragraph of my document?

❶ Click the **Normal view** icon (☰) to switch to Normal view.

❷ Click **Tools**.

❸ Click **Options**.

❹ On the **View** tab, click here and select a value of at least .5".

❺ Click **OK**.

● Word displays the Style Area at the left side of your document.

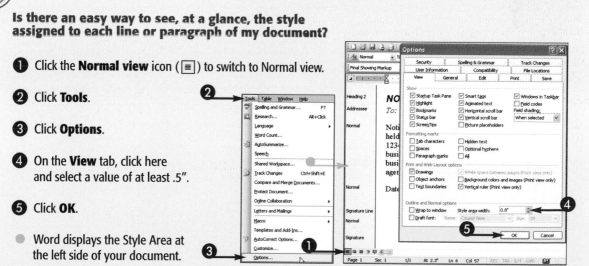

Switch Styles

You can easily change all text that is formatted in one style to another style. Using this technique can help you maintain formatting consistency in your documents.

Switch Styles

1 Select one example of text containing the formatting that you want to change.

2 Click ⚌ to display the Styles and Formatting task pane.

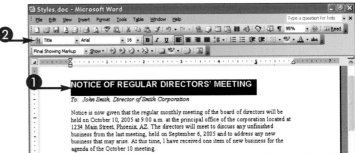

Word displays the Styles and Formatting task pane.

● The style for the selected text appears here.

● Available formatting styles appear here.

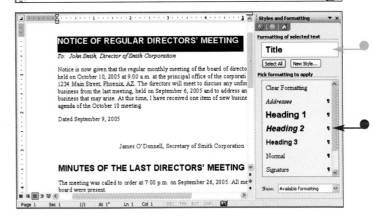

③ Click **Select All**.

● Word selects all text in your document formatted using the style of the text you selected in step **1**.

④ Click the style you want to apply to all selected text.

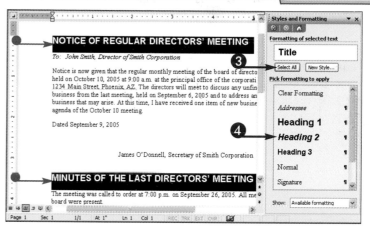

● Word changes all selected text to the style you selected in step **4**.

⑤ Click anywhere to continue working.

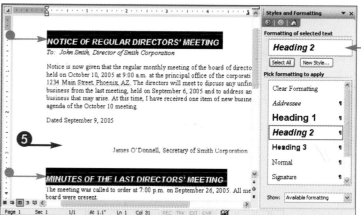

TIPS

What should I do if I do not see the style that I want to use?

You have two choices. First, click the **Show** ⏷ and click **All Styles** to view the built-in styles as well as the styles in use in your document. If you still do not see the style you want to use, you can create it; see the section "Save Formatting in a Style."

What should I do if an existing style is close to what I want, but not quite exactly what I want?

You can change the style's formatting; see the section "Modify a Style" for details. Or, you can apply the style that is close to what you want and then manually adjust the text to make it look exactly the way you want.

Save Formatting in a Style

You can easily create your own styles to store formatting information if you cannot find a built-in style that exactly suits your needs.

You can create character, paragraph, table, and list styles.

1 Click ![icon] to display the Styles and Formatting task pane.

● If any formatted text appears close to the way you want it, select it; some of the text's formatting appears here.

2 Click **New Style.**

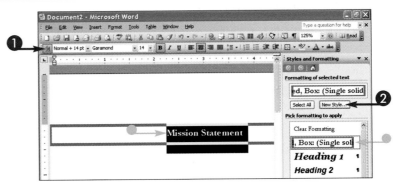

The New Style dialog box appears.

3 Type a name for the style.

4 Click here and select the type of style – **Character**, **Paragraph**, **Table**, or **List**.

This example uses **Paragraph**.

5 Click here and select the style of the paragraph that follows the style you are creating.

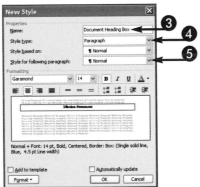

6 Click here and select the font formatting options for the style.

7 Select paragraph alignment, spacing, and indentation options.

8 To use the style in all new documents you create, click the **Add to template** option (changes to).

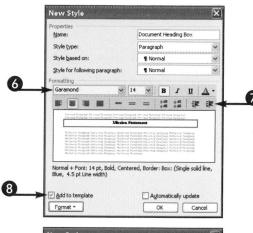

● To specify additional formatting, click **Format**, then select the type of formatting.

Word displays a dialog box where you can add more formatting characteristics to the style.

9 Click **OK** to close that dialog box and redisplay the New Style dialog box.

10 Click **OK** in the New Style dialog box.

Word saves your style; it appears in the Styles and Formatting task pane.

Note: To use the Style, see the section "Apply Formatting Using Styles."

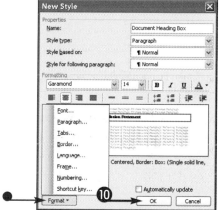

What do the different kinds of styles control?

Character styles control font style, size, and enhancements such as boldface or underlining. Paragraph styles control text alignment, spacing, tab stops, and borders. Paragraph styles can include character styles. Table styles control the appearance of table fonts, borders, shading, and alignment. List styles control alignment and numbering or bullet appearance in lists.

Do I have to create the styles that appear in the Styles and Formatting task pane?

No. Word comes with built-in styles that contain commonly used formatting. Some of the built-in styles serve special purposes; for example, you can automatically build a table of contents using entries styled in Heading 1 through Heading 9. Create a style only when you cannot find a built-in one that suits your needs.

At some point you may decide that the formatting of an existing style is close to but not exactly what you want. You do not need to create a new style; modify the existing one.

Modify a Style

1 Open a document containing the style you want to change.

2 Click 🔏 to display the Styles and Formatting task pane.

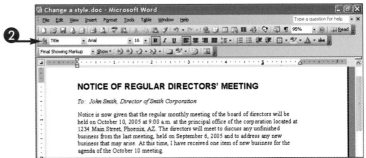

The Styles and Formatting task pane appears.

3 Place ☖ over the style you want to change.

☑ appears.

4 Click ☑ to display a list of options.

5 Click **Modify**.

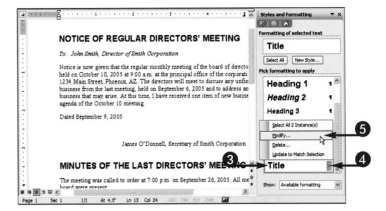

The Modify Style dialog box appears.

6 Select any font formatting or paragraph formatting changes you want to make.

7 Click the **Add to template** option to make the modified style available in new documents (☐ changes to ☑).

8 Click **OK**.

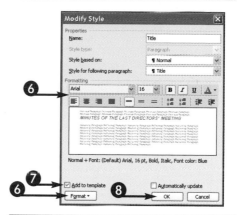

● Word changes all text formatted with the style to incorporate the changes.

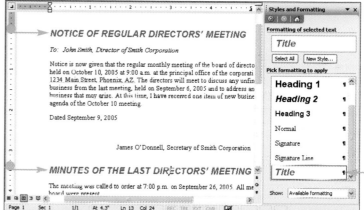

What does the Style based on option do?

Every style you create is based on a built-in Word style. Changing a built-in style can result in many styles changing. For example, many styles are based on the Normal style. If you change the font of the Normal style, you change the font of all styles based on the Normal style.

What does the Automatically update option in the Modify Style dialog box do?

This option (☐ changes to ☑), available only for paragraph styles, causes Word to change a style definition if you apply manual formatting to a paragraph assigned to this style. Because you may not realize that Word is changing the style's definition, this option is recommended or experienced users only.

CHAPTER 7

Format Pages

In addition to applying formatting to characters and paragraphs, you can apply formatting to pages of your Word document. In this chapter find out how to get your page to look its best.

Adjust Margins

You can adjust the right, left, top, and bottom margins of your document. When you adjust margins, Word sets the margins for the entire document.

Word sets the left and right margins to 1.25 inches and the top and bottom margins to 1 inch.

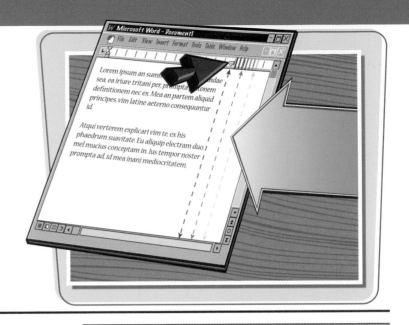

Adjust Margins

1 Click anywhere in the document or section where you want to change margins.

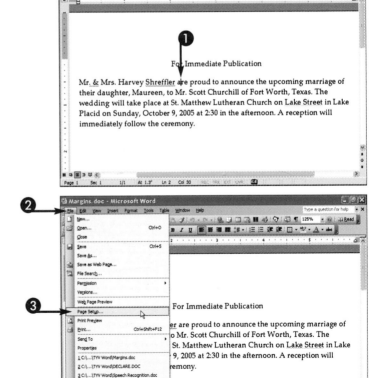

2 Click **File**.

3 Click **Page Setup**.

The Page Setup dialog box appears.

④ Click the **Margins** tab.

● The current margin settings appear here.

⑤ Drag the mouse (I) over any margin.

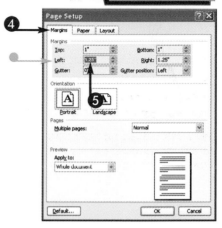

⑥ Type a new margin setting.

⑦ Repeat steps **5** to **6** for each margin setting.

⑧ Click **OK**.

Word saves your changes.

TIPS

Can I change the margins for just one part of my document?

Yes, you can if you divide your document into sections using section breaks. You can set distinct margins for each section of a document. See the section "Insert a Section Break."

Can I use the mouse to change margins?

Yes. In Print Layout view, margins appear blue. Move the mouse into the Ruler area, between the white and blue portions of the ruler. $\text{\textbackslash}$ changes to $\leftrightarrow$ or $\updownarrow$. Drag $\leftrightarrow$ or $\updownarrow$ to reposition the margin.

Insert a Page Break

You can insert a page break to force Word to start text on a new page. Word automatically starts a new page when the current page becomes filled with text.

You insert a page break when you want to control where a new page begins.

Insert a Page Break

① Click the location where you want the text to appear on a new page.

② Click **Insert**.

③ Click **Break**.

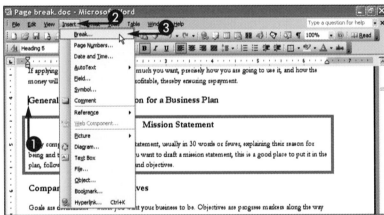

The Break dialog box appears.

④ Click **Page break** (○ changes to ⦿).

⑤ Click **OK**.

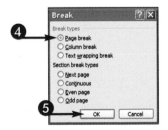

● Word inserts a page break and moves all text after the page break onto a new page.

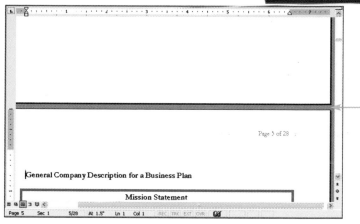

⑥ Click the **Normal view** icon (▤) to see the document in Normal view.

● Word displays a page break line that represents the page break.

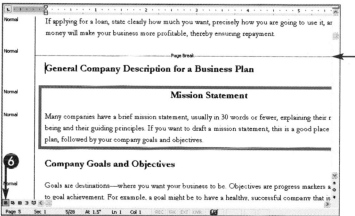

TIPS

Is there a faster way to insert a page break?
Click the location where you want text to appear on a new page and press Ctrl + Enter .

Can I delete a page break?
Yes. You can delete page breaks that you insert into your document; you cannot delete the page breaks Word inserts when a page fills with text. Click ▤ to display the document in Normal view. Click the **Page Break** line and then press Delete .

Control Text Flow and Pagination

You can control the placement of the automatic page breaks that Word inserts when you fill a page with text.

You can eliminate widows and orphans, keep an entire paragraph on one page, keep one paragraph with the next paragraph on a page, or insert a page break before a paragraph.

① Select the text whose flow you want to affect.

Note: To control widows and orphans, you do not need to select any text.

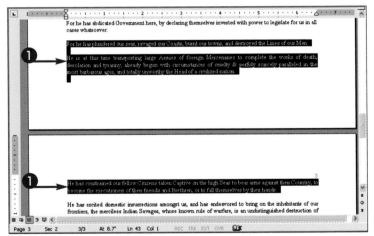

② Click **Format**.

③ Click **Paragraph**.

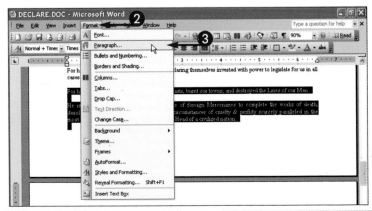

The Paragraph dialog box appears.

4 Click the **Line and Page Breaks** tab.

● This area contains the options you can use to control text flow and automatic pagination.

5 Click an option (☐ changes to ☑).

6 Click **OK** to save your changes.

Word groups the selected text in the manner you specified.

TIPS

What is a widow?

Widow is the term used to describe when the first line of a paragraph appears at the bottom of a page and subsequent lines appear on the following page. Widows are distracting to reading comprehension.

What is an orphan?

Orphan is the term used to describe when the last line of a paragraph appears at the top of a new page and all preceding lines appear at the bottom of the previous page. Like widows, orphans are distracting to reading comprehension.

Align Text Vertically on the Page

You can align text between the top and bottom margins of a page if the text does not fill the page. For example, centering text vertically often improves the appearance of short business letters or report cover pages.

By default, Word applies vertical alignment to your entire document, but you can limit the alignment to a particular section if you divide the document into sections. See the section "Insert a Section Break" For more information.

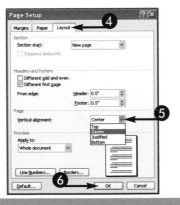

Align Text Vertically on the Page

① Click anywhere on the page you want to align vertically.

② Click **File**.

③ Click **Page Setup**.

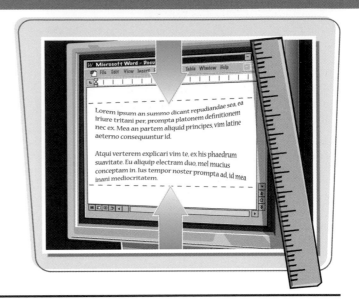

The Page Setup dialog box appears.

④ Click the **Layout** tab.

⑤ Click the **Vertical alignment** ☑ and select a vertical alignment choice.

⑥ Click **OK**.

Word saves your selection.

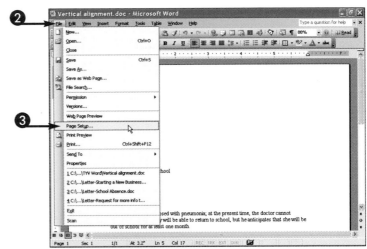

Change Page Orientation

You can change the direction that text prints on a page from the standard portrait orientation of 8½ inches x 11 inches to landscape orientation of 11 inches x 8½ inches.

To remember the difference between the orientations, think of paintings. Leonardo da Vinci painted his famous Mona Lisa portrait with the canvas oriented vertically. Georges Seurat painted his famous Sunday Afternoon on the Island of La Grande Jatte landscape with the canvas oriented horizontally.

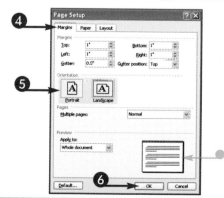

Change Page Orientation

① Click anywhere in the document.

Note: *By default, Word changes the orientation for the entire document. To change orientation for only part of a document, divide the document into sections. See the section "Insert a Section Break."*

② Click **File**.

③ Click **Page Setup**.

The Page Setup dialog box appears.

④ Click the **Margins** tab.

⑤ Select an orientation.

● A preview of your document's orientation appears here.

⑥ Click **OK**.

Word saves your changes.

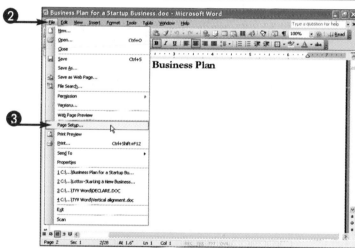

Insert a Section Break

You can insert a section break in a document to establish different margins, headers, footers, vertical page alignment, and other page formatting settings in different portions of your document.

Insert a Section Break

1 Click in the location where you want to start a new section in your document.

2 Click **Insert**.

3 Click **Break**.

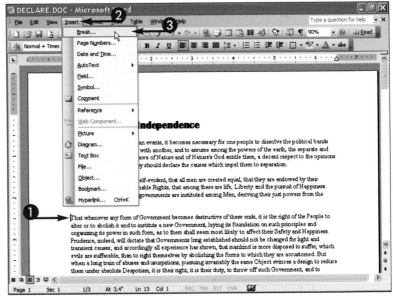

The Break dialog box appears.

4 Click an option to select the type of section break you want to insert (◯ changes to ⦿).

5 Click **OK**.

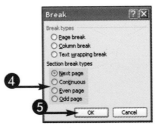

● Word inserts the type of break you selected.

6 Click 🔳 to display the document in Normal view.

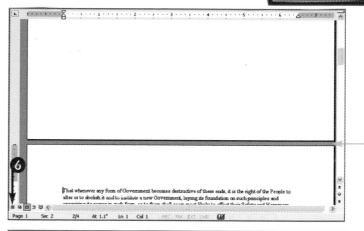

● A section break line appears.

● You can remove the section break by clicking the section break line and pressing the `Delete` key on your keyboard.

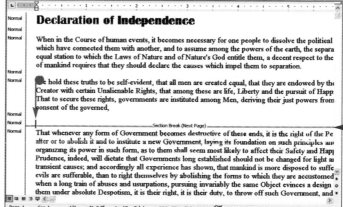

Declaration of Independence

When in the Course of human events, it becomes necessary for one people to dissolve the political which have connected them with another, and to assume among the powers of the earth, the separa equal station to which the Laws of Nature and of Nature's God entitle them, a decent respect to the of mankind requires that they should declare the causes which impel them to separation.

We hold these truths to be self-evident, that all men are created equal, that they are endowed by the Creator with certain Unalienable Rights, that among these are life, Liberty and the pursuit of Happ That to secure these rights, governments are instituted among Men, deriving their just powers from consent of the governed,

―――――Section Break (Next Page)―――――

That whenever any form of Government becomes destructive of these ends, it is the right of the Pe alter or to abolish it and to institute a new Government, laying its foundation on such principles and organizing its power in such form, as to them shall seem most likely to affect their Safety and Happ Prudence, indeed, will dictate that Governments long established should not be changed for light an transient causes; and accordingly all experience has shown, that mankind is more disposed to suffe evils are sufferable, than to right themselves by abolishing the forms to which they are accustomed when a long train of abuses and usurpations, pursuing invariably the same Object evinces a design them under absolute Despotism, it is their right, it is their duty, to throw off such Government, and

---

TIPS

How does Word handle printing when I insert a section break?

Section breaks are formatting marks that do not print; instead, the effects of the section break are apparent when you print. For example, if you insert a **Next Page** section break (○ changes to ◉), Word starts the text that immediately follows the section break on a new page.

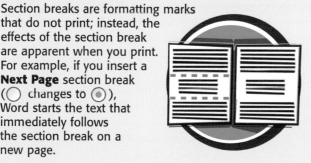

What happens if I select Even page or Odd page?

Word starts the next section of your document on the next even or odd page. If you insert an **Even page** section break (○ changes to ◉) on an odd page, Word leaves the odd page blank. Similarly, if you insert an **Odd page** section break (○ changes to ◉) on an even page, Word leaves the even page blank.

Add Page Numbers to a Document

You can have Word automatically print page numbers on the pages of your document. As you edit your document to add or remove text, Word adjusts the document and the page numbers accordingly.

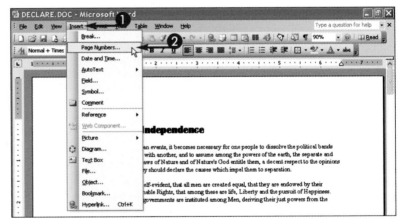

Add Page Numbers to a Document

① Click **Insert**.

② Click **Page Numbers**.

The Page Numbers dialog box appears.

③ Click here and select a location on the page for the page number.

● You can remove the check from this box (☑ changes to ☐) to hide the page number on the first page of the document.

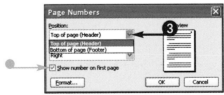

④ Click here and select the position on the line for the page number.

● You can preview the options you select here.

⑤ Click **OK**.

⑥ Click the **Print Layout** icon (▣) to display the document in Print Layout view.

● The page number appears in the location you selected.

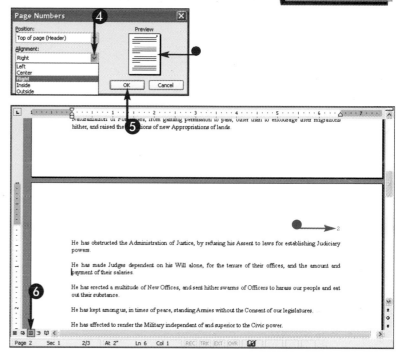

TIP

How can I start each section of my document with Page 1?

If your company's style calls for each chapter starting on Page 1, you can break the document into sections and use these steps to start each section on Page 1.

① Place the insertion point in the first section of your document and complete steps **1** to **4**.

② Click **Format**.

③ In the Page Numbering section, click **Start at** and type **1** in the box.

④ Click **OK** twice.

⑤ Repeat these steps for each subsequent section of your document.

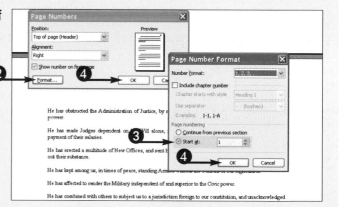

Add Line Numbers to a Document

You can add numbers to the left edge of every line of your document. Line numbers are particularly useful for proofreading; proofreaders can refer to locations in the document by their line numbers.

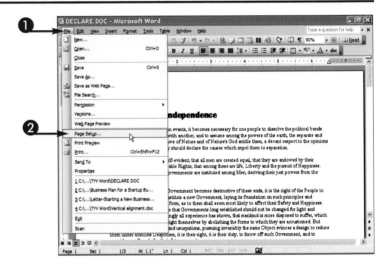

Add Line Numbers to a Document

① Click **File**.

② Click **Page Setup**.

The Page Setup dialog box appears.

③ Click the **Layout** tab.

④ Click **Line Numbers**.

The Line Numbers dialog box appears.

5 Click **Add line numbering** (☐ changes to ☑).

● You can specify line numbering options here.

6 Click an option (○ changes to ◉) to specify whether line numbering should be continuous or start over on each page or section.

7 Click **OK** twice.

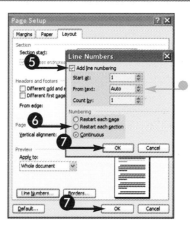

8 Click 🔳 to view the document in Print Layout mode.

● Line numbers appear in the left margin of the document.

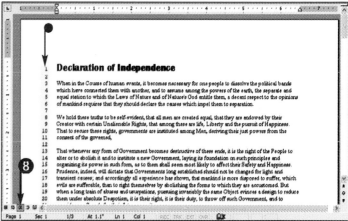

TIPS

What does the From text option control in the Line Numbers dialog box?

Using this option, you can specify the position in inches in the left margin where line numbers will appear. Exercise caution, however; if you specify too large a distance, the line numbers will not appear or print.

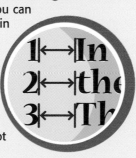

How do I remove line numbers?

Follow steps **1** to **5**; when you click the **Add line numbering**, ☑ changes to ☐, turning off line numbering. Click **OK** twice to save your changes.

Add a Header or Footer

You can use headers at the top of the page and footers at the bottom of the page to add information that you want to appear on each page of your document.

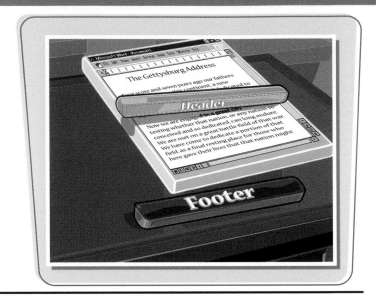

Add a Header or Footer

① Click **View**.

② Click **Header and Footer**.

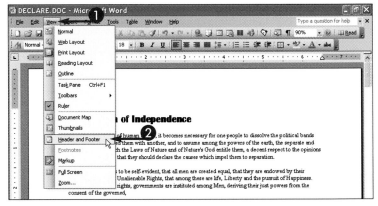

● The Header and Footer toolbar appears.

● The text in your document appears dimmed, and the insertion point appears in the Header box.

③ To add a header, type in the Header box.

Note: *The Header box contains two predefined tabs so that you can center or right-align text.*

④ Click the **Switch Between Header and Footer** icon (🗐) to switch to the footer box.

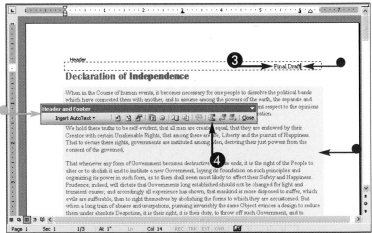

The Footer box appears.

5 To add a footer, type in the Footer box.

● You can switch back to the Header box by clicking again.

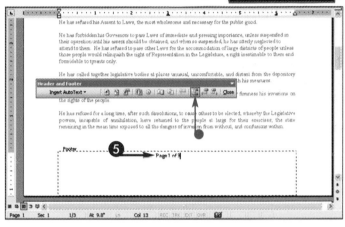

6 Click **Close**.

Word saves your header and footer.

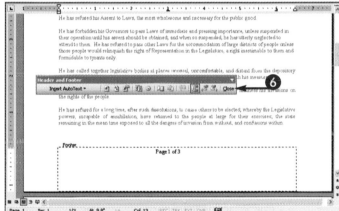

TIP

Can I format text in a header or footer?

Yes. You can apply boldface, italics, underlining, and other character formatting the same way that you apply them in the body of a document. You also can use the icons on the Header and Footer toolbar to format header and footer text. The date and time information you insert updates itself each time you print your document.

Button	Function
🔢	Inserts the current page number
➕	Inserts the number of pages in the document
📅	Inserts the current date
🕐	Inserts the current time

Using Different Headers or Footers Within a Document

You can use different headers or footers in different portions of your document. If you plan to use more than two headers or footers, insert section breaks before you begin. See the section "Insert a Section Break" for details.

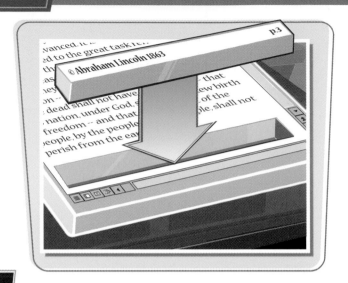

Using Different Headers or Footers Within a Document

① Click in the first section for which you want to create a header or footer.

② Click **View**.

③ Click **Header and Footer**.

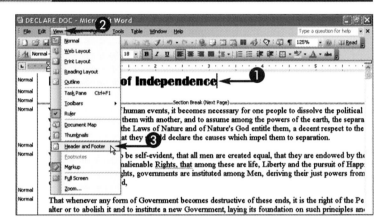

● The Header and Footer toolbar appears.

The text in your document appears dimmed, and the insertion point appears in the Header – Section 1 box.

④ Type in the Header-Section 1 box.

⑤ Click 🖳.

You switch to the Footer-Section 1 box.

⑥ Type a footer.

⑦ Click the **Show Next** icon (🖳) to switch to the header or footer for the next section.

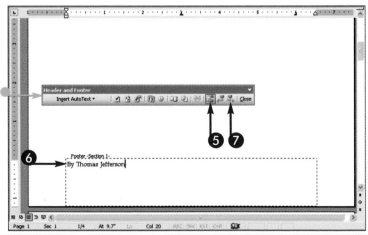

- The Header-Section 2 or Footer-Section 2 box appears.

- Word identifies the header or footer as Same as Previous.

8 Click the **Link to Previous** icon (🔲) to unlink the headers or footers.

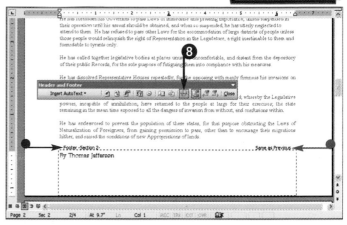

- Word unlinks the headers or footers and removes the "Same as Previous" marking from the header or footer.

9 Type the text you want to appear in this section's header or footer.

10 Repeat steps **7** to **9** for each section for which you want a different header or footer.

- You can switch between the Header box and the Footer box by clicking 🔲 at any time.

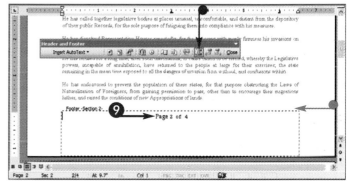

TIP

Can I create different headers or footers for odd or even pages?

Yes, and you do not need to insert section breaks.

1 Complete steps **2** to **3** in this section.

2 On the Header and Footer toolbar, click the **Page Setup** icon (🔲).

3 Click the **Different odd and even** option (☐ changes to ☑).

4 Click **OK**.

- Each header or footer box is renamed to Odd Page or Even Page.

5 Type in the Odd Page Header box or click 🔲 to type a footer.

6 Click 🔲 to switch to the Even Page Header box or the Even Page Footer box.

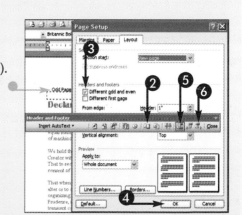

Add a Footnote or Endnote

You can add footnotes or endnotes to a document to provide additional explanatory information or to cite references to other works.

Footnotes are numbered 1, 2, 3, and appear within your document. Endnotes are numbered i, ii, iii, and appear at the end of your document.

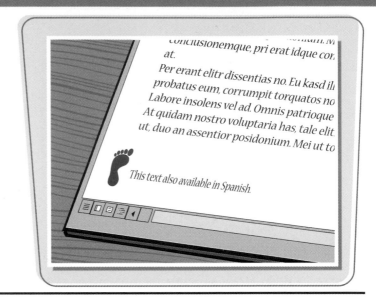

① Click 🔲 to display the document in Print Layout view.

② Click in the document where you want the footnote or endnote number to appear.

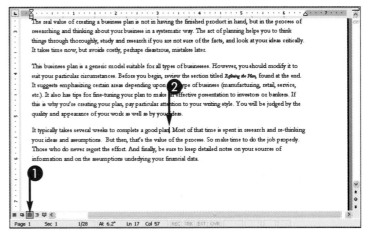

③ Click **Insert**.

④ Click **Reference**.

⑤ Click **Footnote**.

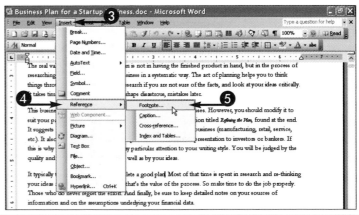

The Footnote and Endnote dialog box appears.

6 Click an option to specify whether you want to insert footnotes or endnotes (○ changes to ◉).

7 Click **Insert**.

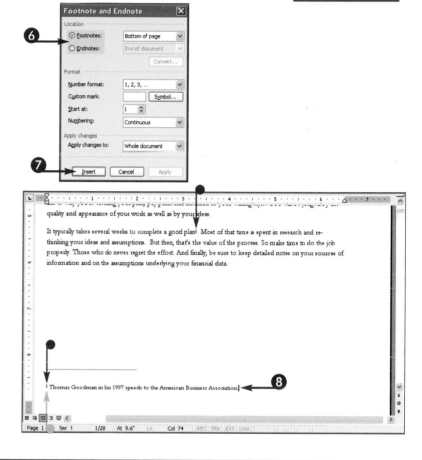

● Word displays the footnote or endnote area.

8 Type the text for the footnote or endnote.

● The number for the footnote or endnote appears both in the body of the document and in the note.

quality and appearance of your work as well as by your ideas.

It typically takes several weeks to complete a good plan[1]. Most of that time is spent in research and re-thinking your ideas and assumptions. But then, that's the value of the process. So make time to do the job properly. Those who do never regret the effort. And finally, be sure to keep detailed notes on your sources of information and on the assumptions underlying your financial data.

[1] Thomas Goodman in his 1997 speech to the American Business Association.

TIP

Is there anything I can do if I change my mind and want to use endnotes instead of footnotes?

Yes, you can convert footnotes to endnotes or endnotes to footnotes.

1 Complete steps **3** to **5** in this section.

2 Click **Convert**.

3 In the Convert Notes dialog box, click **OK**.

4 The Cancel button changes to Close; click **Close**.

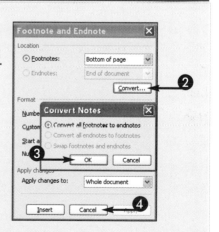

View, Edit, or Delete Footnotes or Endnotes

Working in any view, you can view footnote or endnote text, modify the text, or delete the footnote or endnote.

View, Edit, or Delete Footnotes or Endnotes

VIEW FOOTNOTES OR ENDNOTES

① Position the mouse ⌶ over the footnote or endnote number in your document.

The mouse ⌶ changes to 🔲.

● A ScreenTip appears, displaying the footnote or endnote text.

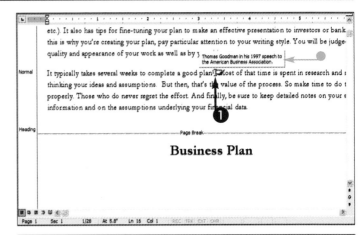

EDIT FOOTNOTES OR ENDNOTES

① Double-click the footnote or endnote reference number in your document.

● In Print Layout view, Word moves the insertion point into the footnote or endnote.

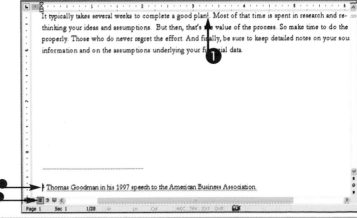

● In Normal view, Word displays the footnote or endnote in the Footnotes pane.

❷ Edit the text of the note as needed.

❸ Click **Close** when you finish editing.

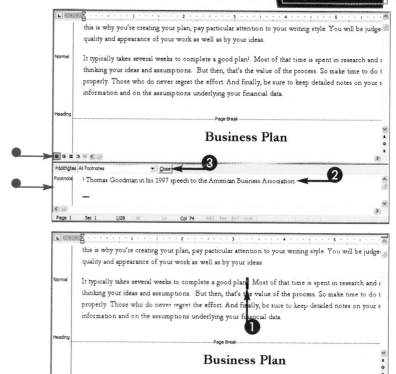

DELETE A FOOTNOTE OR ENDNOTE

❶ Select the number of the footnote or endnote you want to delete.

❷ Press **Delete** on your keyboard.

Word removes the footnote or endnote number and related information from the document and automatically renumbers subsequent footnotes or endnotes.

TIP

Can I print endnotes on a separate page?

❶ Click in your document immediately before the first endnote.

❷ Click **Insert**.

❸ Click **Break**.

❹ In the Break dialog box, click the **Page break** option (◯ changes to ◉).

❺ Click **OK**.

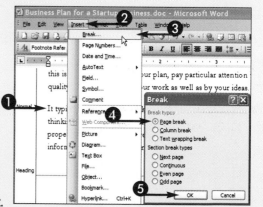

Word inserts a page break immediately before the endnotes, placing them on a separate page at the end of your document.

Generate a Table of Contents

You can automatically create a table of contents that updates as you update your document. Table of contents entries can come from headings in your document or from text you mark to appear in the table of contents.

This section uses text styled as Heading 1 and Heading 2 to create table of contents entries.

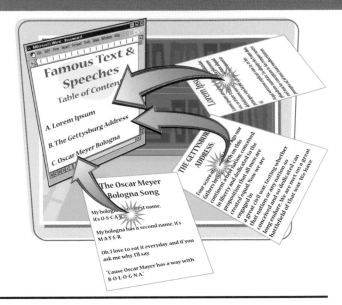

Generate a Table of Contents

① Toward the top of the document, create a separate page for the table of contents.

Note: See the section "Insert a Page Break" for details.

② Place the insertion point on a blank line below the page title.

③ Click **Insert**.

④ Click **Reference**.

⑤ Click **Index and Tables.**

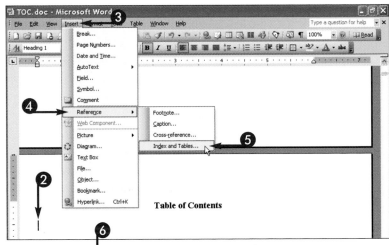

The Index and Tables dialog box appears.

⑥ Click the **Table of Contents** tab.

● This area shows a preview of the table of contents.

● These options control the appearance of page numbers.

● You can click the **Tab leader** ▾ to select the character that appears between an entry and its page number.

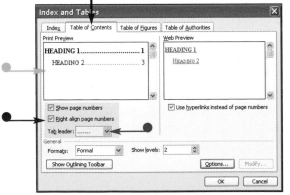

7 Click here and select a format for the table of contents.

● Word updates the preview of the table of contents based on your selection.

● You can click here to control the number of heading styles Word includes in the table of contents.

8 Click **OK**.

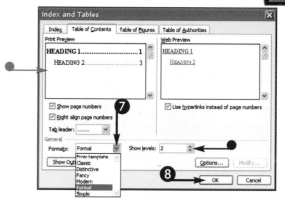

● Word inserts a table of contents into your document.

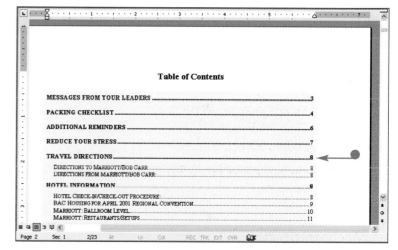

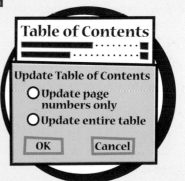

How do I update the table of contents if I find typographical errors or add more text to the document?

You should correct typographical errors in the body of the document, not in the table of contents. After changing your document, click anywhere in the table of contents; the text appears highlighted in gray. Press F9 and select the option to update page numbers only or both text and page numbers and click **OK**.

You can add a watermark, which is faint text that appears behind information in a document, to your document to add interest or convey a message.

Watermarks are visible in Print Layout view and when you print your document.

Add a Watermark

1 Click ⊞ to display your document in Print Layout view.

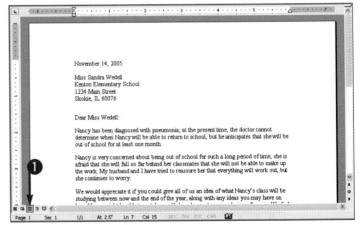

November 14, 2005

Miss Sandra Wedell
Kenton Elementary School
1234 Main Street
Skokie, IL 60076

Dear Miss Wedell:

Nancy has been diagnosed with pneumonia; at the present time, the doctor cannot determine when Nancy will be able to return to school, but he anticipates that she will be out of school for at least one month.

Nancy is very concerned about being out of school for such a long period of time; she is afraid that she will fall so far behind her classmates that she will not be able to make up the work. My husband and I have tried to reassure her that everything will work out, but she continues to worry.

We would appreciate it if you could give all of us an idea of what Nancy's class will be studying between now and the end of the year, along with any ideas you may have on

2 Click **Format**.

3 Click **Background**.

4 Click **Printed Watermark**.

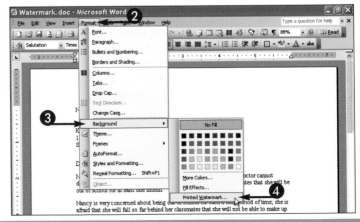

The Printed Watermark dialog box appears.

5 Click the **Text watermark** option
(○ changes to ⦿).

6 Click here and select the text to use as a watermark.

● You can use these options to control the font, size, color, intensity, and layout of the watermark.

7 Click **OK**.

● Word displays the watermark on each page of your document.

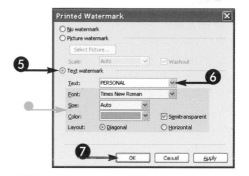

What happens if I click Picture watermark option in the Printed Watermark dialog box?
Word enables you to select a picture stored on your hard drive to act as the watermark in your document.

1 Follow steps **1** to **5**, selecting **Picture watermark** in step **5**.

2 In the Printed Watermark dialog box, click **Select Picture**.

3 In the Insert Picture dialog box, navigate to the location on your hard drive containing the picture you want to use as a watermark.

4 Click **Insert**.

5 Click **OK** to add the picture watermark to your document.

Add a Page Border

You can add a border around each page of your document to add interest to the document.

1 Click 🔲 to display your document in Print Layout view.

2 Click **Format**.

3 Click **Borders and Shading**.

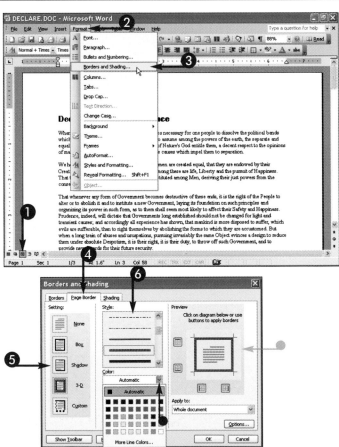

The Borders and Shading dialog box appears.

4 Click the **Page Border** tab.

5 Click the type of border you want to add to your document.

6 Click a style for the border line.

● This area shows a preview of the border.

● You can click here to select a color for the border.

● You can click here to select a width for the border.

7 Click here to specify the pages on which the border should appear.

8 Click **OK**.

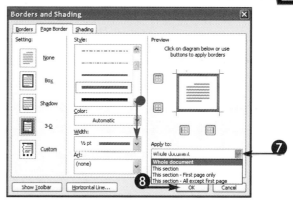

● Word applies the border you specified.

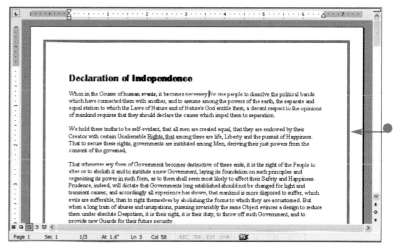

TIP

Can I add a border that does not surround the page?

Yes. Follow these steps:

1 Follow steps **1** to **7** to select the border you want to apply.

2 In the Preview area, click the border lines that you do not want to appear in your document.

3 Click **OK**.

Word applies the modified page border.

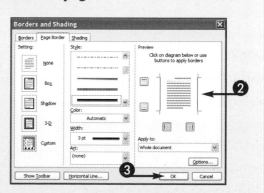

Apply a Theme

If you intend to view your document on-screen or on the Internet, you can apply a theme to the document to enhance its appearance.

Themes appear only in Print Layout, Web Layout, and Reading Layout views, and some elements of themes, such as backgrounds, do not print.

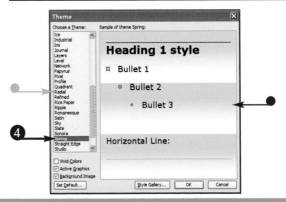

Apply a Theme

① Click 🔲 to display the document in Print Layout view.

② Click **Format**.

③ Click **Theme**.

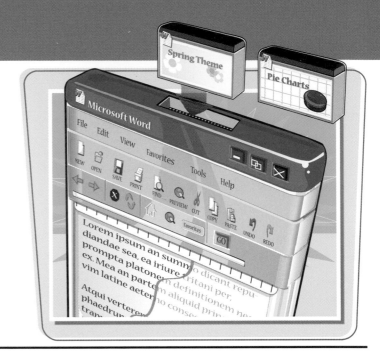

The Theme dialog box appears.

● The list of available themes appears here.

④ Click a theme.

● A preview of the theme appears here.

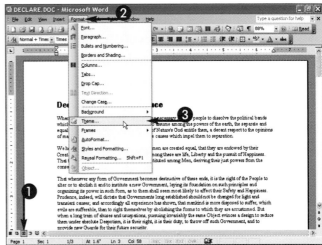

5 Repeat step **4** until you find a theme you want to use.

6 Click **OK**.

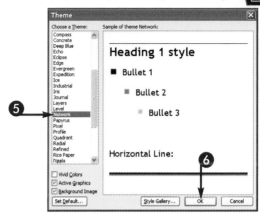

Word applies the theme to your document.

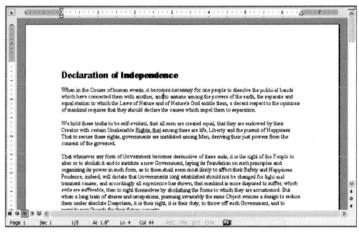

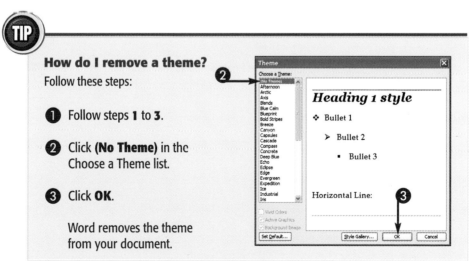

How do I remove a theme?
Follow these steps:

1 Follow steps **1** to **3**.

2 Click **(No Theme)** in the Choose a Theme list.

3 Click **OK**.

Word removes the theme from your document.

Create Newspaper Columns

You can format text in your document so that it appears in columns like the text in newspapers. Newspaper column formatting is useful when you are creating newsletters or brochures.

Text appears in newspaper columns only in Print Layout view.

Create Newspaper Columns

① Click 🔲 to display your document in Print Layout view.

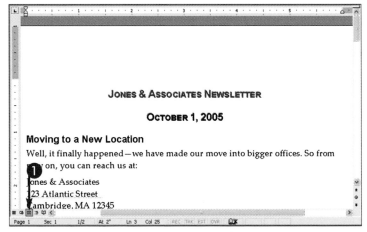

② Click **Format**.

③ Click **Columns**.

The Columns dialog box appears.

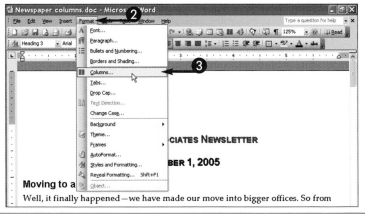

④ Click the number of columns you want to create.

● You can use these settings to change the width of each column and the spacing between columns.

● You can click the **Line between** option (☐ changes to ☑) to add a line between columns.

● A preview appears here.

⑤ Click **OK**.

Word applies the column settings.

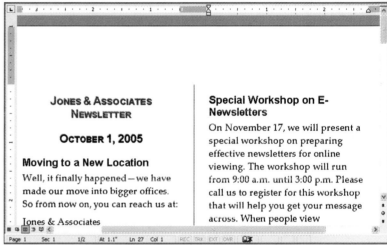

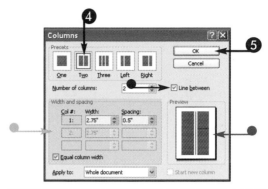

JONES & ASSOCIATES
NEWSLETTER

OCTOBER 1, 2005

Moving to a New Location

Well, it finally happened—we have made our move into bigger offices. So from now on, you can reach us at:

Jones & Associates

Special Workshop on E-Newsletters

On November 17, we will present a special workshop on preparing effective newsletters for online viewing. The workshop will run from 9:00 a.m. until 3:00 p.m. Please call us to register for this workshop that will help you get your message across. When people view

---

TIP

Can I force text from the left column to the top of the next column?

Yes. You can insert a column break.

① Click at the left edge of the text you want to appear at the top of the second column.

② Click **Insert**.

③ Click **Break**.

④ Click **Column break** (◯ changes to ◉).

⑤ Click **OK**.

Word forces a break.

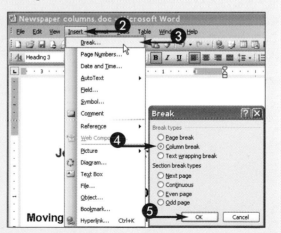

CHAPTER 8

Print Documents

Now that your document looks the way you want it to look, you are ready to distribute it. In this chapter, you learn how to preview and print documents, print envelopes, and print labels.

Preview a Document Before Printing

You can preview your document before printing it to look for layout errors and other possible formatting inconsistencies.

① Click **File**.

② Click **Print Preview**.

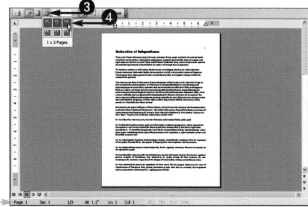

Your document appears in the Print Preview window.

● You can identify the page in your document using the Status bar.

③ To view more than one page at a time, click the **Multiple Pages** icon (▦) and drag the mouse pointer (↖) across the number of pages you want to view.

④ Click when the number of pages appears.

Word displays the number of pages you selected.

● You can click the **One Page** icon (▦) to redisplay only one page.

⑤ To magnify an area of a page, place ↖ over the area (↖ changes to ⊕).

⑥ Click the area.

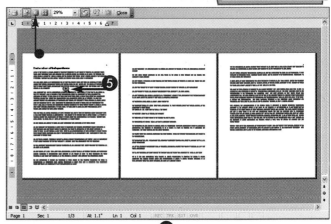

Word magnifies the area.

⑦ Click **Close** to close the Print Preview window.

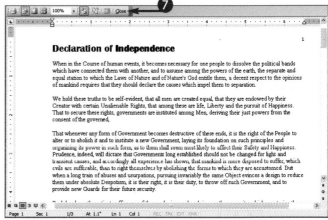

Declaration of **Independence**

When in the Course of human events, it becomes necessary for one people to dissolve the political bands which have connected them with another, and to assume among the powers of the earth, the separate and equal station to which the Laws of Nature and of Nature's God entitle them, a decent respect to the opinions of mankind requires that they should declare the causes which impel them to separation.

We hold these truths to be self-evident, that all men are created equal, that they are endowed by their Creator with certain Unalienable Rights, that among these are life, Liberty and the pursuit of Happiness. That to secure these rights, governments are instituted among Men, deriving their just powers from the consent of the governed,

That whenever any form of Government becomes destructive of these ends, it is the right of the People to alter or to abolish it and to institute a new Government, laying its foundation on such principles and organizing its power in such form, as to them shall seem most likely to affect their Safety and Happiness. Prudence, indeed, will dictate that Governments long established should not be changed for light and transient causes; and accordingly all experience has shown, that mankind is more disposed to suffer, while evils are sufferable, than to right themselves by abolishing the forms to which they are accustomed. But when a long train of abuses and usurpations, pursuing invariably the same Object evinces a design to reduce them under absolute Despotism, it is their right, it is their duty, to throw off such Government, and to provide new Guards for their future security.

TIPS

I tried to magnify an area on Page 2 while viewing three pages and the mouse pointer did not change to ⊕. What did I do wrong?

You can magnify an area of a page only while viewing one page at a time. Click ▦ to redisplay only one page, click ▾ to find the page to view, and then complete steps **5** to **6**.

Can I edit my document while previewing it?

Magnify your document and then click the **Magnifier** icon (▨). The ⊕ changes to I and you can edit.

Print a Document

If your computer is connected to a printer that is turned on, you can print your document to produce a paper copy of it.

1 Click **File**.

2 Click **Print**.

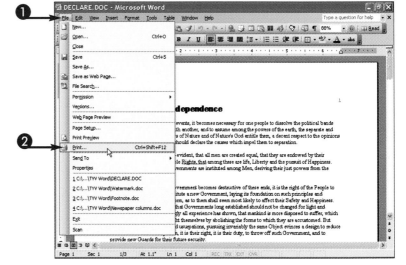

The Print dialog box appears.

● If you have more than one printer available, you can click here and select a printer.

3 Click a Page Range option to identify the pages you want to print (◯ changes to ◉).

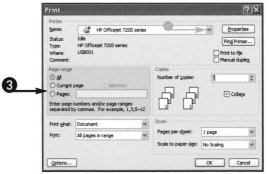

④ To print more than one copy, type the number of copies to print here.

⑤ Click here and select what you want to print.

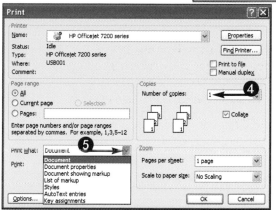

● You can click the Print ▾ to print odd or even pages instead of all pages.

● You can use this option to specify the number of pages you want to print on each sheet of paper.

● You can use this option to adjust the document to fit on a selected paper size.

⑥ Click **OK**.

Word prints your document using the options you selected.

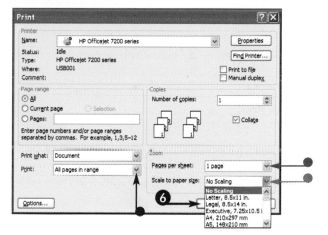

 TIPS

How can I print only certain text in my document?

Select the text before starting these steps. In step **3**, click **Selection**, which will be available because you selected text.

Can I print noncontiguous pages of my document?

Yes. Follow steps **1** to **3**, clicking the **Pages** option (○ changes to ⦿) in step **3**. In the Pages box, type the pages you want to print, such as **1,3,4,7-9**.

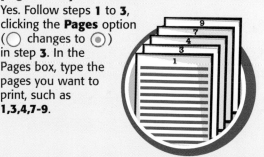

Change the Paper Size and Source

You can change the paper size on which you print your document and the paper source. For example, you may want to print on legal-sized paper that your printer stores in a separate paper tray.

❶ Click **File**.

❷ Click **Page Setup**.

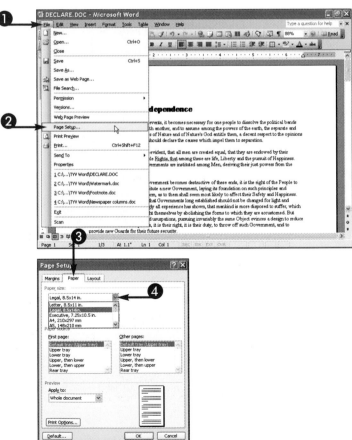

The Page Setup dialog box appears.

❸ Click the **Paper** tab.

❹ Click here and select the paper size you want to use.

- The height and width of the paper size you selected appear here.

- A preview of your selection appears here.

- You can use these options to change the paper source.

⑤ Click a location here for the source of paper for the first page you print.

⑥ Click a location here for the source of paper for the rest of the document.

⑦ Click **OK**.

Word saves your changes.

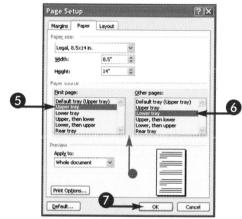

TIP

Can I print part of my document on one paper size and another part on a different paper size?

Yes. But you must first insert section breaks in your document for each portion you want to print on different paper sizes per the instructions in Chapter 7. Next, follow these steps.

① Place ⌕ in the section you want to print on a different paper size.

② Follow steps **1** to **6** in this section.

③ In the Page Setup dialog box, click the Apply to ☑ and click **This section**.

④ Click **OK**.

⑤ Repeat the process for other sections of the document.

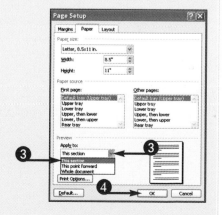

Print an Envelope

If your printer supports printing envelopes, Word can print a delivery and return address on an envelope for you.

Consult your printer manual to determine if your printer supports printing envelopes.

① Click **Tools**.

② Click **Letters and Mailings**.

③ Click **Envelopes and Labels**.

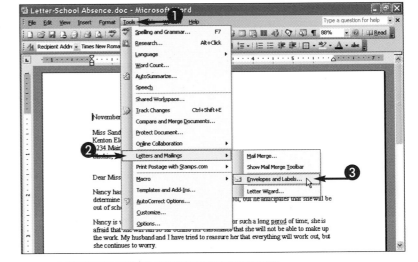

The Envelopes and Labels dialog box appears.

④ Click the **Envelopes** tab.

Note: If Word finds an address near the top of your document, it enters that address in the Delivery address box.

⑤ You can type a delivery address.

You can remove an existing address by selecting it and pressing `Delete` on your keyboard.

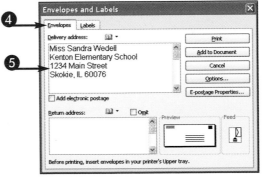

By default, Word displays no return address in the Return address box.

6 Click here to type a return address.

7 Click **Print**.

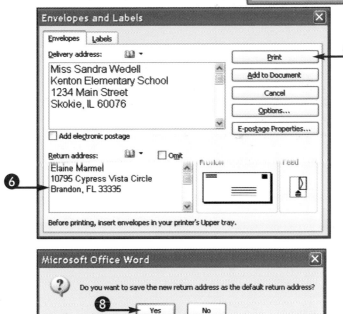

This dialog box appears if you supplied a return address.

Note: If you save the return address, Word displays it each time you print an envelope.

8 Click **Yes**.

Word saves the return address as the default return address.

What happens if I click the Options button?
Word displays the Envelope Options dialog box. On the Envelope Options tab, you can set the envelope size, include a delivery bar code, and set fonts for the delivery and return addresses. On the Printing Options tab, you can set the feed method and tray for your printer.

Print Labels

You can format a Word document so that you can use it to type labels. For example, you can create address, name tag, and file folder labels.

This section demonstrates how to create a blank page of address labels onto which you can type address label information.

① Click **Tools**.

② Click **Letters and Mailings**.

③ Click **Envelopes and Labels**.

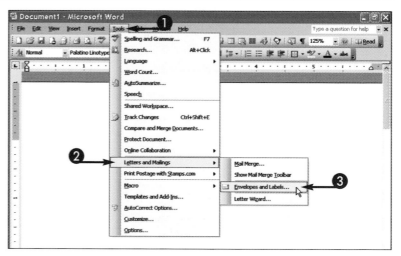

The Envelopes and Labels dialog box appears.

④ Click the **Labels** tab.

● This area shows the label currently selected.

⑤ Click **Options**.

The Label Options dialog box appears.

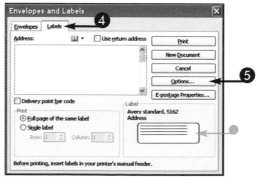

6 In this area, select the type of printer and printer tray to print labels.

7 Click here to select the maker of your labels.

8 Click the product number of your labels.

● The label information appears here.

9 Click **OK** to save your selections.

10 Click **New Document**.

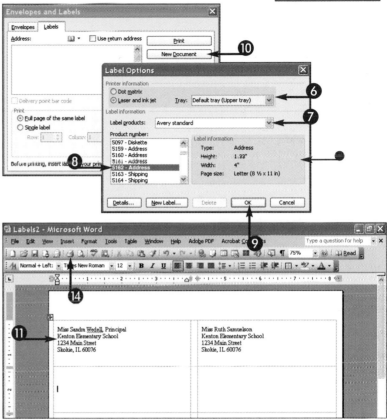

Word displays a blank document, set up to hold label information.

11 Type a label.

12 Press `Tab` to move from label to label.

13 Repeat steps **11** to **12** for each label you want to print.

14 Click the **Print** icon ().

Word prints the labels.

TIP

Can I print a single label?

1 Complete steps **1** to **4** in this section to open the Envelopes and Labels dialog box.

2 Click the **Single label** option (○ changes to ◉).

3 Use these boxes to type the row and column of the label you want to use on the label sheet.

4 Type the label information here.

5 Click **Print**.

Word prints the single label.

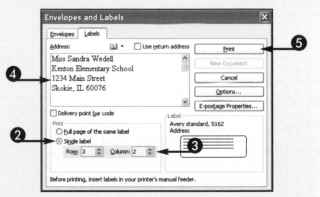

Work with Tables

Do you want to keep the information in your Word document easy to read? The answer may very well be to add a table to contain your data. In this chapter, you learn how to create and work with tables in Word.

You can create a table and enter text into it. Tables are well suited to organize and display larges amounts of data.

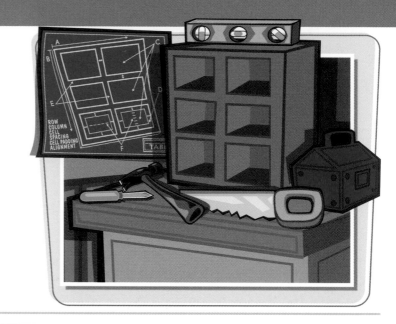

SET UP A TABLE

① Click in your document where you want the table to appear.

② Click the **Insert Table** icon (▦) to display a table grid.

③ Move the mouse pointer (↖) across the squares that represent the number of rows and columns you want in your table.

Note: You can always add rows or columns to your table later.

④ Click the square representing the lower right corner of your table.

The table appears in your document.

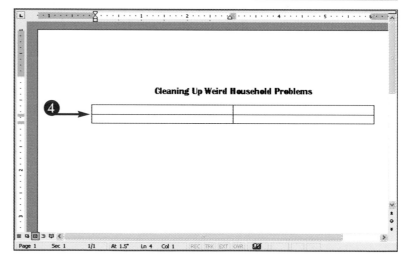

5 Click in the table cell where you want to enter information.

6 Type the information; if necessary, Word expands the row size to accommodate the text.

You can press `Tab` to move the insertion point to the next cell.

7 Repeat steps **5** to **6** until you enter all of the table's text.

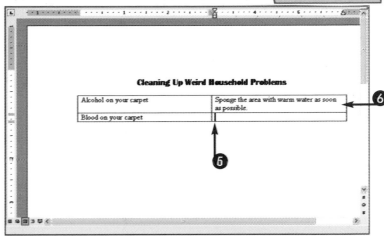

DELETE A TABLE

1 Click anywhere in the table you want to delete.

2 Click **Table**.

3 Click **Delete**.

4 Click **Table**.

Word removes the table and its contents from your document.

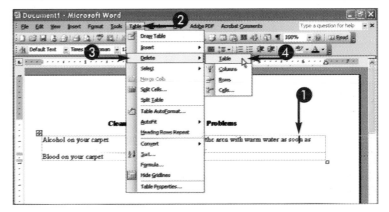

TIPS

Can I add rows to the bottom of the table?

Yes, you can easily add rows to the bottom of a table by placing the insertion point in the last cell of the table and pressing the `Tab` key.

What, exactly, is a table cell?

A cell is the name of the square that appears at the intersection of a row and a column. In spreadsheet programs, columns are named with letters, rows are named with numbers, and a cell is named using the column letter and row number. For example, the cell at the intersection of Column A and Row 2 is called A2.

Change the Row Height or Column Width

You can change the height of rows or the width of columns to accommodate your table information.

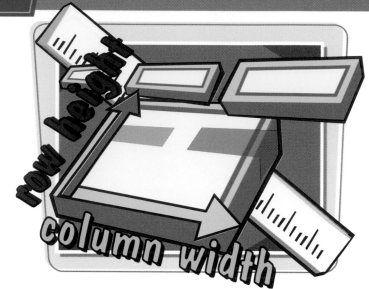

CHANGE THE ROW HEIGHT

1. Click the Print Layout icon (▣) to display the document in Print Layout view.

2. Position the mouse I over the bottom of the row (I changes to ↕).

3. Drag the row edge up to shorten or down to lengthen the row height.

● A dotted line marks the bottom of the row.

4. Release the mouse.

● The new row height appears.

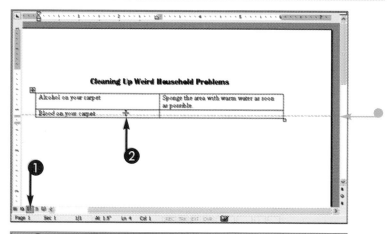

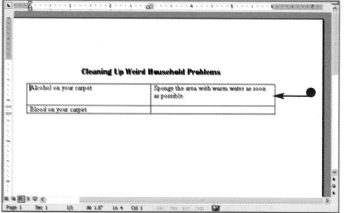

CHANGE THE COLUMN WIDTH

① Click 🔲 to display the document in Print Layout view.

② Position the mouse ⌶ over the right side of the column (⌶ changes to ⊕).

③ Drag the column edge right to widen or left or to narrow the column width.

● A dotted line marks the side of the column.

④ Release the mouse.

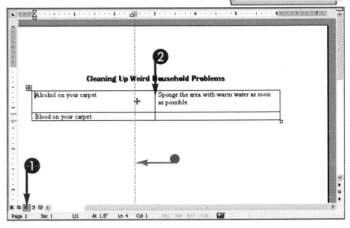

● The new column width appears.

Note: When you change the width of a column, the width of the column to its right also changes. When you change the width of the rightmost column, you change the width of the entire table.

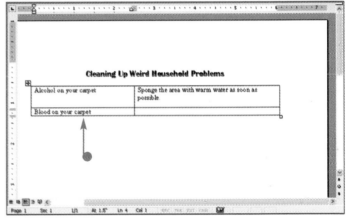

TIPS

I tried to change the row height but the mouse pointer never changed to ╪. What did I do wrong?

You can change row height only when displaying your document in either Print Layout view or Web Layout view. Make sure you select one of those views by clicking the **Print Layout** icon (🔲) or the **Web Layout** icon (🔲).

Is there an easy way I can make a column the size that accommodates the longest item in it?

Yes, you double-click the right edge of the column. Word widens or narrows the column based on the longest entry in the column.

Move a Table

You can move a table to a different location in your document.

❶ Click ▣ to display the document in Print Layout view.

❷ Move the mouse ⌶ over the table.

● A handle (⊞) appears in the upper left corner of the table.

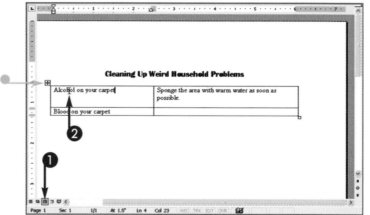

❸ Move the mouse ⌶ over the handle (⌶ changes to ✛).

❹ Drag the table to a new location.

● A dashed line represents the table position.

The table appears in the new location.

Note: To copy the table, perform these steps but press **Ctrl** *in step 4.*

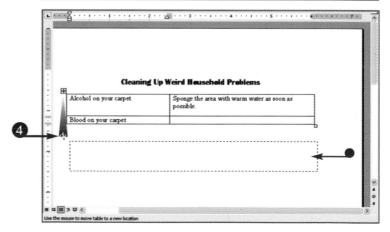

188

If you find that your table dimensions don't suit your purpose, you can resize the table from Print Layout view or Web Layout view. For example, you may want to resize a table to make it longer and narrower.

Resize a Table

① Click 🔲 to display the document in Print Layout view.

② Move the mouse ⌶ over the table.

● A handle (▢) appears in the lower right corner of the table.

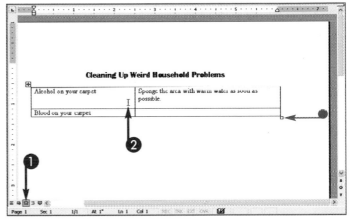

③ Move the mouse ⌶ over the handle (⌶ changes to ↘).

④ Drag the table up to make it smaller or down to make it larger (↘ changes to +).

Note: You can also drag to the left or right as you drag up or down.

A dashed line represents the size of the table.

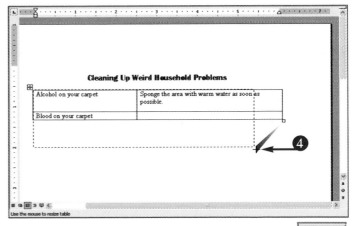

Add or Delete a Row

You can easily add rows to accommodate more information or remove rows or information you do not need.

ADD A ROW

1 Click in the row below where you want a new row to appear.

2 Click **Table**.

3 Click **Insert**.

4 Click **Rows Above**.

● Word inserts a row and selects it.

5 Click in the row to add information to the table.

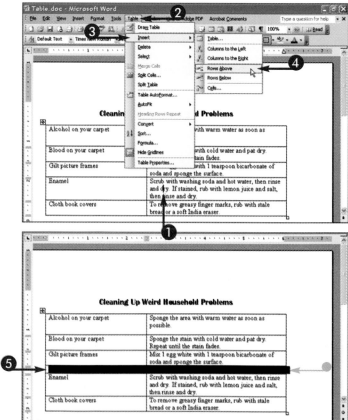

DELETE A ROW

1 Click anywhere in the row you want to delete.

2 Click **Table**.

3 Click **Delete**.

4 Click **Rows**.

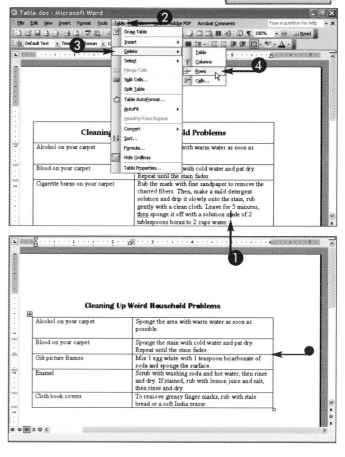

● Word removes the row and any text it contained from the table.

TIPS

Can I delete more than one row at a time?

Yes. Select the rows you want to delete before performing steps **2** to **4** in the subsection "Delete a Row." To select the rows, position I outside the left side of the table (I changes to ▷). Drag to select the rows you want to delete.

Can I insert more than one row at a time?

Yes. Select the number of rows you want to insert before you perform steps **1** to **4** in the subsection "Add a Row." You can select rows below where you want the new rows and then perform steps **1** to **4** or you can select rows above where you want the new rows and, in step **4**, click **Rows Below**.

Add or Delete a Column

You can add or delete columns to change the structure of a table to accommodate more or less information.

When you add columns, Word decreases the size of the other table columns to accommodate the new column.

Add or Delete a Column

ADD A COLUMN

1 Click in the column to the left of the column you want to add.

2 Click **Table**.

3 Click **Insert**.

4 Click **Columns to the Right**.

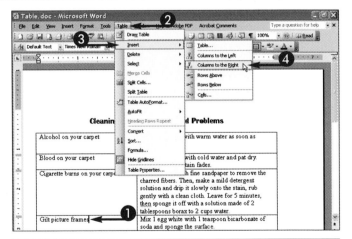

● Word inserts a column in the table to the right of the column you selected and selects the column.

5 Click in the column to add text to it.

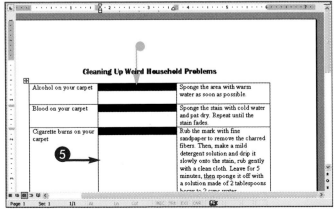

DELETE A COLUMN

1 Click anywhere in the column you want to delete.

2 Click **Table**.

3 Click **Delete**.

4 Click **Columns**.

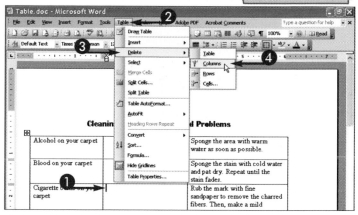

● Word removes the column and any text it contained from the table.

Word does not resize existing columns to use the space previously occupied by the deleted column.

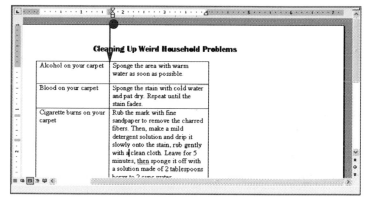

TIP

Is there a way I can easily enlarge a table to fill up the space between the left and right margins after deleting a column?

Yes. Follow these steps:

1 Click anywhere in the table.

2 Click **Table**.

3 Click **AutoFit**.

4 Click **AutoFit to Window**.

The table content and columns readjust to fill the space.

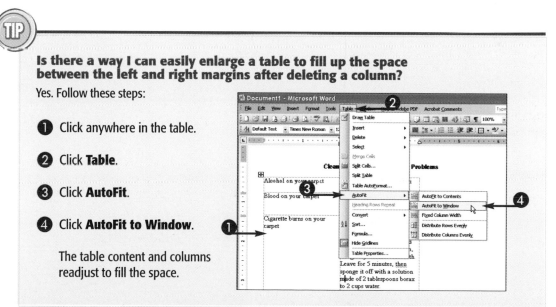

Combine Cells

You can combine two or more cells to create one large cell, in which you can store, for example, a table title.

① Position the mouse I inside the left edge of the first cell you want to merge (I changes to ➤).

② Drag ➤ across the cells you want to merge.

③ Click **Table**.

④ Click **Merge Cells**.

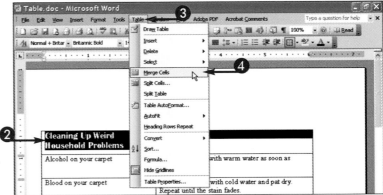

● Word combines the cells into one cell and selects that cell.

⑤ Click anywhere to cancel the selection.

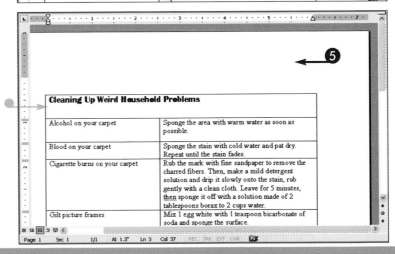

If you find that you have more information in one cell than you want, you can split the cell into two or more cells that span one or more rows, columns, or both to make room for the extra information.

Split Cells

① Click anywhere in the cell you want to split.

② Click **Table**.

③ Click **Split Cells**.

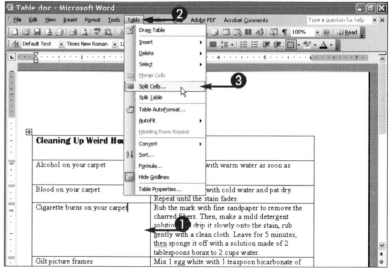

The Split Cells dialog box appears.

④ Type here to reflect the number of columns into which you want to split the cell.

⑤ Type here to reflect the number of rows into which you want to split the cell.

⑥ Click **OK**.

Word splits the cell.

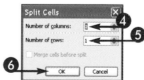

To make your text look more uniform, you can align text or numbers with the top, bottom, left, right, or center of cells.

By default, Word aligns table entries at the top left edge of each cell.

1 Position the mouse I inside the left edge of the cell whose alignment you want to change (I changes to ➚) and drag to select the cell.

2 Click the **Tables and Borders** icon (▦) to display the Tables and Borders toolbar.

3 Click the **Align** icon (▤ ▾) and click the alignment you want to use.

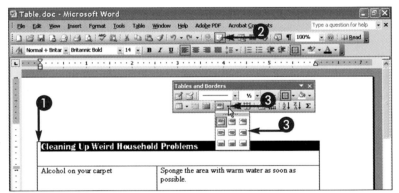

● Word aligns the text accordingly in the cell.

4 Click anywhere to cancel the selection.

5 Click the **Close** icon (✖) to close the Tables and Borders toolbar.

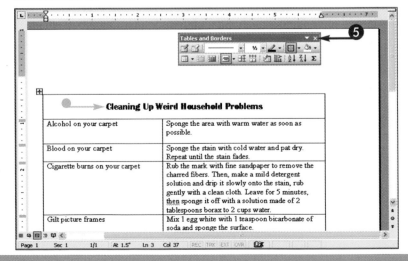

Add Shading to Cells

You can add shading to cells to call attention to them.

Add Shading to Cells

1 Position the mouse I inside the left edge of the cell you want to shade (I changes to ➤) and drag to select the cell.

2 Click ▦ to display the Tables and Borders toolbar.

3 Click the **Shading** icon 🎨 to click a shading color.

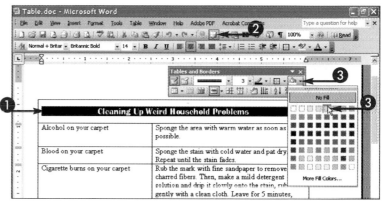

● Word applies the shading to the selected cells.

4 Click anywhere to cancel the selection.

5 Click ✖ to close the Tables and Borders toolbar.

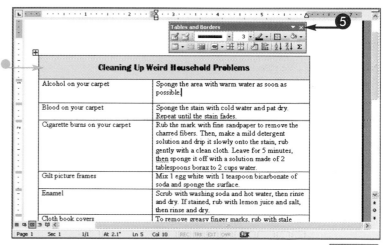

Change Cell Borders

You can add borders to cells to call attention to them.

① Position the mouse I inside the left edge of the cell you want to border (I changes to ➚) and drag to select the cell.

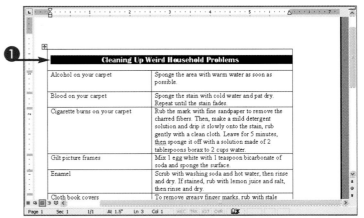

② Click 🔲 to display the Tables and Borders toolbar.

③ Click the **Line Style** 🔽 to display available line styles for the border line.

④ Click the line style you want to apply.

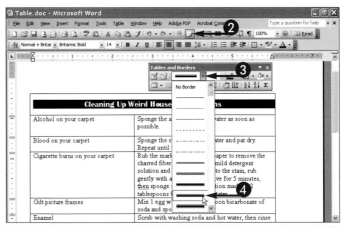

5 Click the **Borders** 🔲▾ icon.

● Border styles appear.

6 Click the type of border to apply.

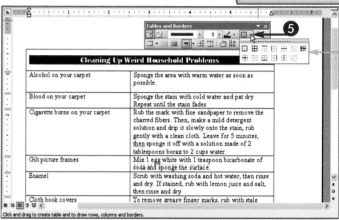

● Word applies the border to the selected cells.

7 Click anywhere to cancel the selection.

8 Click ⊠ to close the Tables and Borders toolbar.

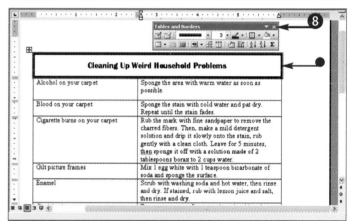

TIP

How can I remove borders from table cells?

1 Complete steps **1** to **2**.

2 Click the **Borders** 🔲▾.

3 Click the **No Border** button (🔲).

Word removes the borders from the table cells.

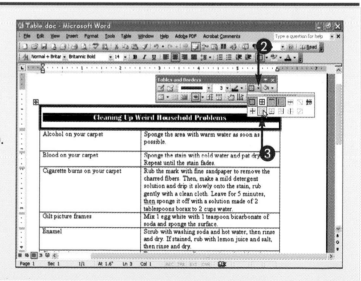

Format a Table

You can apply any number of predefined table styles to a table to format it.

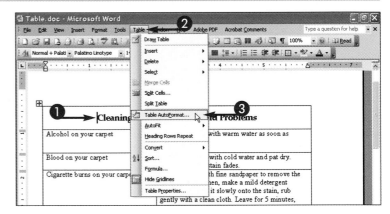

1. Click anywhere in the table.
2. Click **Table**.
3. Click **Table AutoFormat**.

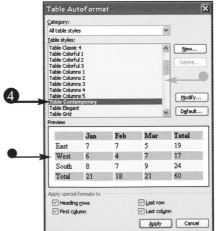

The Table AutoFormat dialog box appears.

● A list of available table styles appears here.

4. Click the table style you want to use.

● A preview of the table style appears here.

● The parts of the table to which Word applies the table style appear here.

❺ Click an option to add (☑) or remove (☐) it from the table style.

❻ Click **Apply**.

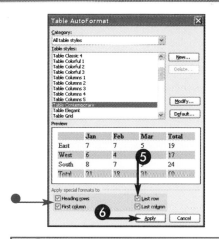

The table appears in the table style you selected.

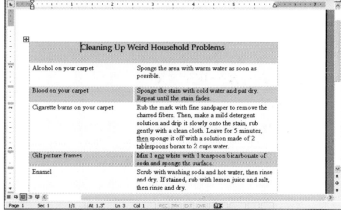

How can I remove a table formatting design?

If you just applied the formatting, you can click the **Undo** icon (↺). If you performed other actions since applying the table formatting design, perform steps **1** to **4**, selecting **Table Grid** as the table style. Then, click **Apply**.

What happens if I click the Default button in the Table AutoFormat dialog box?

A dialog box appears, enabling you to set the selected table style as the default table style. You can set a default table style for all new tables in the current document or for all future new documents. Click an option and then click **OK** to set a default table style; otherwise, click **Cancel**.

Work with Graphics

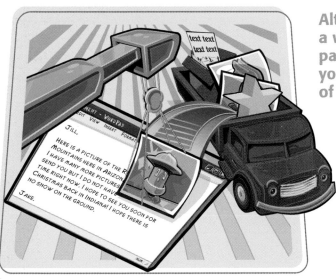

Although Word is primarily a word-processing software package, you can spruce up your documents in a variety of ways using graphics.

Add WordArt

WordArt is decorative text that you can add to a document as an eye-catching visual effect. You can create new WordArt text or apply a WordArt style to existing text.

① Click the location where you want to add WordArt.

You can select existing text and apply WordArt to it.

② Click **Insert**.

③ Click **Picture**.

④ Click **WordArt**.

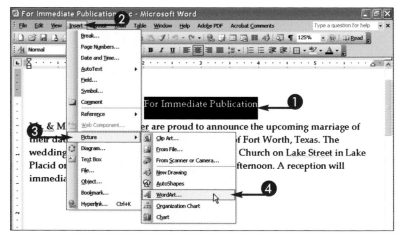

The WordArt Gallery dialog box appears.

⑤ Click the style you want to apply.

⑥ Click **OK**.

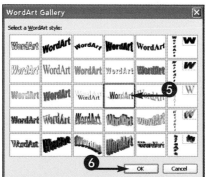

The Edit WordArt Text dialog box appears.

● If you selected text in step **1**, your text appears selected; otherwise, the words "Your Text Here" appear selected.

⑦ If necessary, type the text you want to display using WordArt.

⑧ Click **OK**.

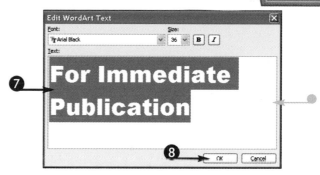

● Word displays text formatted in the selected WordArt style.

Can I edit or delete WordArt?

Yes. To do so, follow these steps:

❶ Click the WordArt text that you want to edit or delete.

● Handles (■) appear around the selected WordArt.

The WordArt toolbar appears.

❷ Press Delete to delete the WordArt or click **Edit Text**.

The Edit WordArt Text dialog box redisplays.

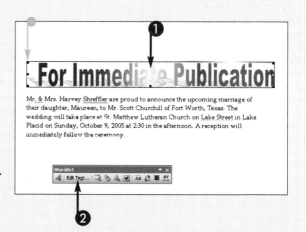

Add a Picture

In a Word document you can include a picture file stored on your computer. This gives your document a professional or personal touch.

Add a Picture

1 Click in your document where you want to add a picture.

2 Click **Insert**.

3 Click **Picture**.

4 Click **From File**.

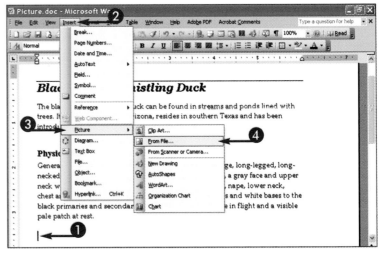

The Insert Picture dialog box appears.

● The folder you are viewing appears here.

● You can click here to navigate to a different folder.

● You can click these icons to navigate to commonly used locations where pictures may be stored.

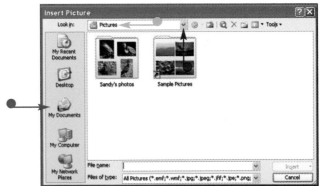

5 Navigate to the folder containing the picture you want to add.

6 Click the picture you want to add to your document.

7 Click **Insert**.

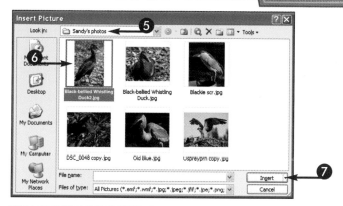

● The picture appears in your document.

Note: *To move or resize a picture, see the section "Move or Resize a Graphic."*

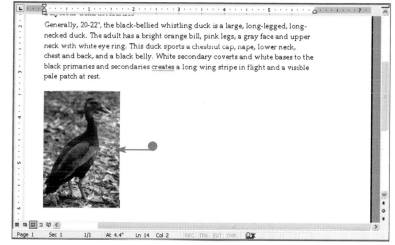

How can I edit or delete a picture?

To quickly edit or delete pictures, follow these steps:

1 Click the picture that you want to edit or delete.

● Handles (■) appear around the selected picture and the Picture toolbar appears.

2 Press Delete to delete the picture or click a button on the Picture toolbar to make changes to the picture.

For example, click the **More Contrast** icon (▣) to increase the contrast in the picture.

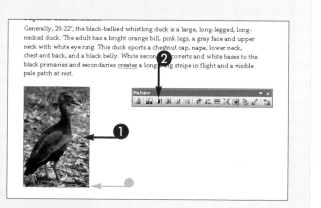

Add a Clip Art Image

You can add clip art images to your document to help get your message across.

You can locate images using the Microsoft Clip Organizer window or by searching for images.

COPY IMAGES FROM THE CLIP ORGANIZER WINDOW

① Click **Insert**.

② Click **Picture**.

③ Click **Clip Art**.

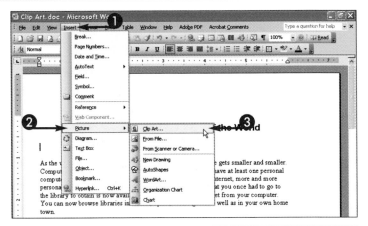

The Clip Art task pane appears.

④ Click the **Organize clips** link.

*Note: The Add Clips to Organizer window appears when you have not cataloged picture, sound, and motion files on your hard disk. Click **Now** to catalog your media files.*

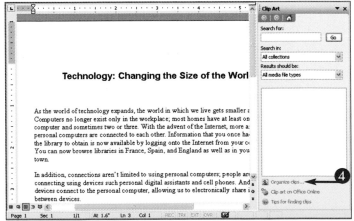

The Microsoft Clip Organizer window appears.

● The Collection List displays folders containing clip art images. A plus sign (⊞) beside a folder means that additional folders appear inside the folder.

5 Click ⊞ beside a folder to display the folders inside it (⊞ changes to ⊟).

6 Click a folder or ⊞ beside the folder.

Clip art images in the folder appear here.

7 Click the image you want to add to your document.

8 Click the **Copy** icon (📋).

Word copies the image to the clipboard.

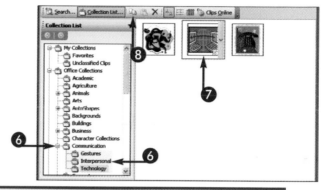

How can I copy more than one image to the clipboard?
To copy more than one image to the clipboard, follow these steps:

1 Complete steps **1** to **4** in this section, clicking your document on the Windows Taskbar.

2 Click **Edit**.

3 Click **Office Clipboard**.

4 Click **Microsoft Clip Organizer** on the Windows Taskbar.

5 Complete steps **5** to **8** for each image you want available; then complete steps **9** to **11**.

6 Click an image in the Office Clipboard pane to add it to your document.

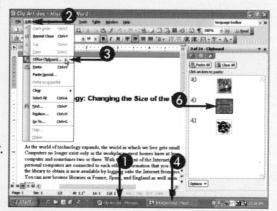

continued

Add a Clip Art Image *(continued)*

When you locate an image using the Microsoft Clip Organizer window, you copy one you want to the Windows clipboard so that you can paste it into your document.

⑨ Click the **Close** icon (🗙) to close the Microsoft Clip Organizer.

A message appears, asking if you want to make the image you copied to the clipboard available after closing the Microsoft Clip Organizer.

⑩ Click **Yes**.

Your document reappears.

⑪ Click in the location where you want the image to appear.

⑫ Click the **Paste** icon (📋).

● The image appears in your document.

● You can click 🗙 to close the Clip Art task pane.

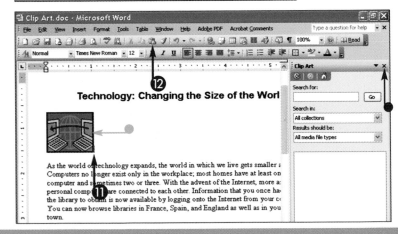

SEARCH FOR CLIP ART IMAGES

1 If you closed the Clip Art task pane, complete steps **1** to **3** in the subsection "Copy Images from the Clip Organizer Window."

2 Click here and type one or more words to describe the image you want to find.

3 Click **Go**.

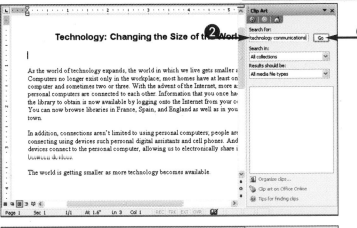

● Images matching the words you typed appear here.

4 Click in your document where you want to place the image.

5 Click an image.

● The image appears in your document.

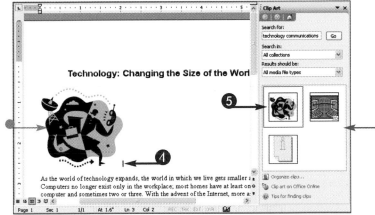

TIPS

What happens if I click the Search in ?

You have the opportunity to limit the search to specific collections. Searching takes less time if you limit the search, but the search may not display as many clip art images if you limit it.

What is a collection?

A collection is a group of clip art images that are related. Office Collections contains clip art images available on your hard drive or on your Office CD. Web Collections contains images available at Microsoft Office Online; you must be connected to the Internet to use Web Collections.

Add an
AutoShape

To give your Word document pizzazz, you can add shapes such as lines, arrows, stars, and banners — called AutoShapes — to your document.

AutoShapes are visible only in Print Layout, Web Layout, and Reading Layout views.

Add an AutoShape

① Right-click any toolbar.

② Click **Drawing**.

● The Drawing toolbar appears at the bottom of the screen.

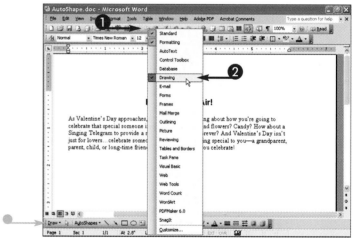

③ Click **AutoShapes**.

④ Click the type of AutoShape you want to add to your document.

⑤ Click a shape.

- Word adds a drawing canvas to your document where you can add, move, and size graphics.

6 Position the mouse (⊞) at the upper left corner of the place where you want the AutoShape to appear.

7 Drag the mouse ⊞ down and to the right until the AutoShape is the size you want.

- When you release the mouse button, the AutoShape appears.

- The handles (☐) surrounding the AutoShape indicate that the AutoShape is selected.

You can use these handles to move or resize the AutoShape.

Note: See the section "Move or Resize a Graphic" for details.

You can press **Esc** to hide the drawing canvas.

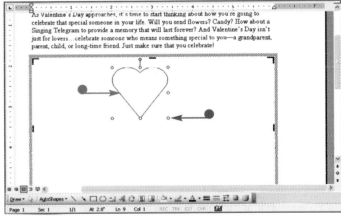

How do I delete an AutoShape?

To delete the shape entirely, you must delete the drawing canvas. To do this, you simply click outside the AutoShape, but inside the drawing canvas. Handles surrounding the AutoShape disappear, but the edge of the drawing canvas remains visible. You can then press **Delete** to delete the AutoShape and the drawing canvas. If you press **Delete** while the handles appear around the AutoShape, Word deletes the AutoShape but leaves the drawing canvas. You can then place a different AutoShape on the drawing canvas using steps **3** to **7**.

Add a Text Box

You can add a text box to your document to control the placement of text.

Text boxes are visible only in Print Layout, Web Layout, and Reading Layout views.

Add a Text Box

1 Right-click any toolbar.

2 Click **Drawing**.

● The Drawing toolbar appears at the bottom of the screen.

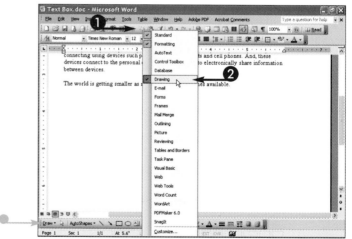

3 Click the **Text Box** icon (⊡).

● Word adds a drawing canvas to your document where you can add, move, and size graphics.

● The mouse pointer changes to +.

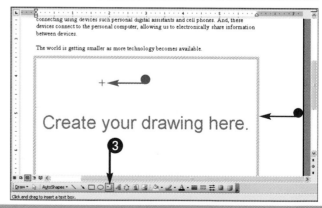

④ Position the mouse + at the upper left corner of the place where you want the text box to appear.

⑤ Drag the mouse + down and to the right until the text box is the size you want.

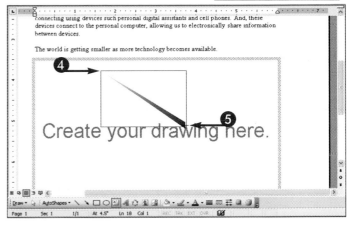

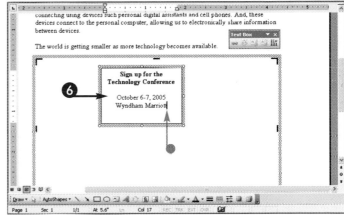

● When you release the mouse button, the text box and the Text Box toolbar appear, and the insertion point appears in the text box.

⑥ Type the text you want to appear in the text box.

Note: *You can format the text the same way you format any text in Word. See Chapter 5 for details.*

You can press Esc to hide the drawing canvas.

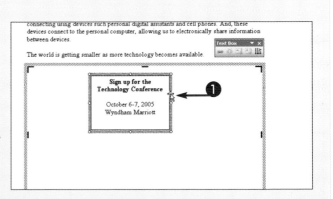

How do I delete a text box?
Follow these steps:

❶ Click any edge of the text box.

The border of the text box changes.

❷ Press Delete.

The text box disappears from the drawing canvas.

To delete the drawing canvas, click any edge and press Delete.

Move or Resize a Graphic

If you find that a graphic is not positioned where you want it or if it is too large or too small, you can move and resize pictures, ClipArt images, AutoShapes, and text boxes.

Move or Resize a Graphic

MOVE A GRAPHIC

① Click the graphic.

● Handles (⬚ or ▪) surround the graphic.

② Position the mouse I over the picture or ClipArt image or over the edge of the AutoShape or text box (I changes to ↖ or ✛).

③ Drag the graphic to a new location.

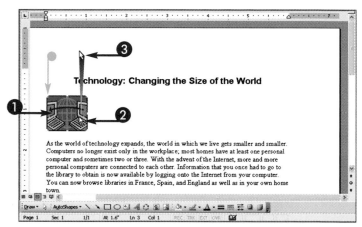

A dashed line may appear, indicating the new location of the graphic.

● The graphic appears in the new location.

④ Click outside the graphic to cancel its selection.

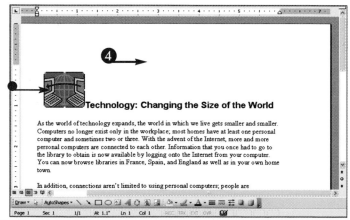

216

RESIZE A GRAPHIC

1 Click the graphic.

● Handles (☐ or ■) surround the graphic.

2 Position the mouse I over one of the handles
(I changes to ↗, ↔, ↘, or ↕).

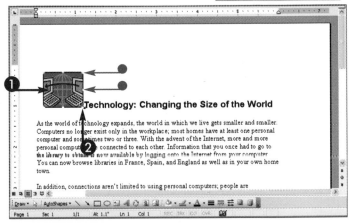

3 Drag the handle until the graphic is the
appropriate size.

● A dashed line indicates the new size of
the graphic.

The graphic appears in the new size.

4 Click outside the graphic to cancel its selection.

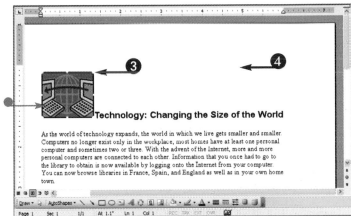

**Is there an easy way I can make a
graphic move only horizontally or
vertically but not diagonally?**

Yes. Press and hold the Shift
key as you drag the graphic.
Word allows you to move
the graphic horizontally or
vertically but not diagonally.

**Does it matter which handle
I use to resize a graphic?**

If you click and drag any of the
corner handles, you maintain
the proportion of the graphic
as you resize it. The handles
on the sides, top, or bottom
of the graphic resize the
width or the height only of
the graphic.

Change the Color of a Graphic

You can add color to an AutoShape or a text box to draw attention to it or to make it more interesting.

1 Display the Drawing toolbar by following steps **1** to **3** in the section "Add an AutoShape."

2 Click the AutoShape or text box to which you want to apply color.

Handles (☐) appear around the image.

3 Click ▼ to display available colors.

4 Click the color you want to apply.

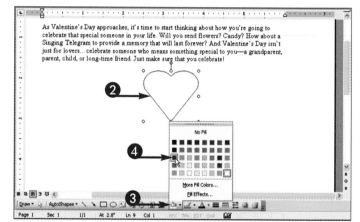

● Word fills the AutoShape or text box with the selected color.

You can press Esc to cancel the selection of the image.

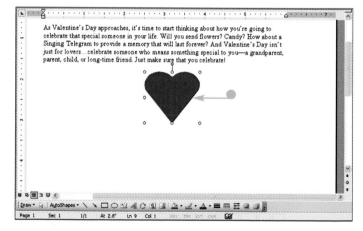

For dramatic effect, you can rotate pictures, clip art images, and some AutoShape images. You cannot rotate text boxes.

Rotate a Graphic

① Click the image you want to rotate.

Handles (⊡ or ⌃) appear around the image.

② Move the mouse ⌶ over the green handle at the top of the image (⌶ changes to ↻).

③ Drag the mouse ⟨⟩ in the direction you want to rotate the image.

● A dotted line marks the image position.

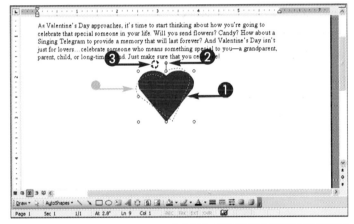

● Word displays the rotated image.

You can press Esc to cancel the selection of the image.

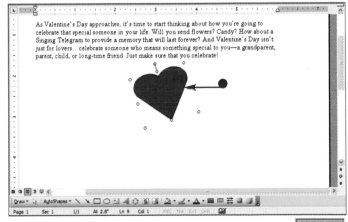

Add a Shadow to a Graphic

You can add depth to a picture, an AutoShape, or a text box by adding a shadow to it.

You cannot add shadows to most clip art images.

Add a Shadow to a Graphic

1 Display the Drawing toolbar by following steps **1** to **3** in the section "Add an AutoShape."

2 Click the graphic.

Handles (☐ or ☐) appear around the image.

3 Click the **Shadow** icon (☐) to display the available shadow styles.

4 Click a shadow style.

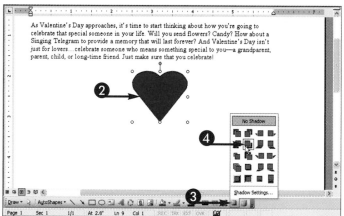

● Word adds the shadow to the graphic.

To remove a shadow, repeat steps **1** to **4**, selecting No Shadow in step **4**.

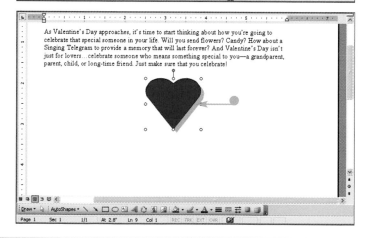

To create an interesting visual effect, you can make a text box or an AutoShape appear three-dimensional.

You cannot make a picture or a clip art image appear three-dimensional.

Make a Graphic Three Dimensional

❶ Display the Drawing toolbar by following steps **1** to **3** in the section "Add an AutoShape."

❷ Click the graphic.

Handles (⊡ or ◪) appear around the image.

❸ Click the **3-D Style** icon (▣) to display the available shadow styles.

❹ Click a 3-D style.

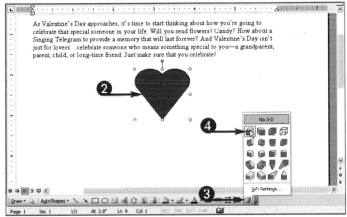

● Word adds the three-dimensional style to the graphic.

To remove a three-dimensional style, repeat steps **1** to **4**, selecting No 3-D in step **4**.

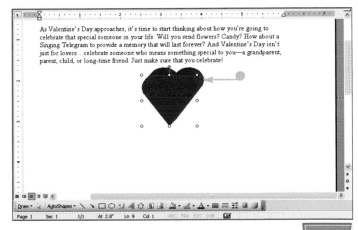

Wrap Text Around a Graphic

You can control the way that Word wraps text around a graphic image in your document.

This becomes very important when you want to place graphics in a document where space is at a premium, such as a two-columned newsletter.

Wrap Text Around a Graphic

1 Click the **Print Layout** icon (▣) to display the document in Print Layout view.

2 Click the graphic.

● Handles (⊙ or ▲) appear around the image.

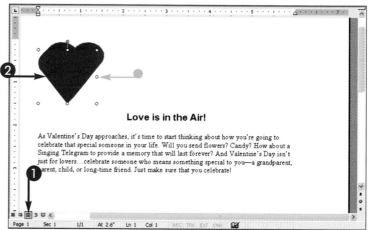

3 Click **Format**.

4 Click the command for the type of graphic you selected, such as AutoShape, Picture, or WordArt.

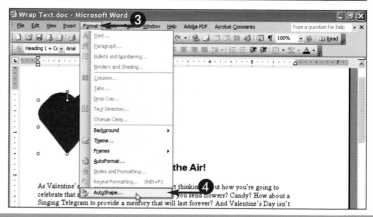

The Format AutoShape dialog box appears.

5 Click the **Layout** tab.

6 Click the wrapping style you want to apply.

7 If appropriate, click the Horizontal alignment you want to apply to the graphic (⚪ changes to ⦿).

8 Click **OK**.

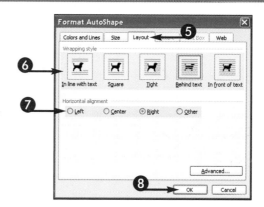

● Word wraps text around the graphic using the settings you specified.

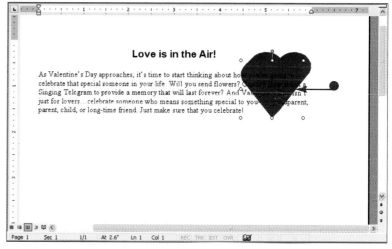

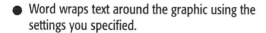

How come I can use Horizontal alignment for some but not all wrapping styles?

You can set horizontal alignment for any graphic that is a floating graphic. By default, Word creates inline graphics that act as text characters. Change a graphic from inline to floating by changing the text-wrapping style to any wrapping style other than In line with text.

What do the various wrapping style settings mean?

Square places the graphic in an imaginary box that fits the graphic's largest dimensions; text wraps around the imaginary box. **Tight** works similarly to **Square**, but text fits tightly around the edges of the actual image, rather than the imaginary box. **Behind text** places the image behind, and showing through, text. **In front of text** places the image in front of text, hiding the text.

Work with Diagrams

You can add an organization chart, or a cycle, radial, pyramid, Venn, or target diagram to your document to illustrate a concept.

Work with Diagrams

ADD A DIAGRAM

1 Click in your document where you want the diagram to appear.

2 Click **Insert**.

3 Click **Diagram**.

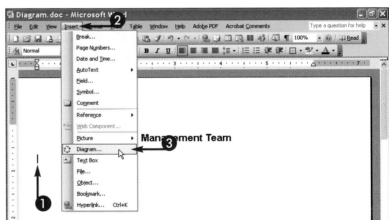

The Diagram Gallery dialog box appears.

4 Click the type of diagram you want to add.

● A description of the selected diagram appears here.

5 Click **OK**.

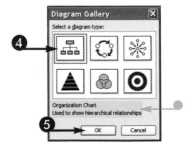

● Word adds the diagram to your document.

● A toolbar for the diagram appears. The toolbar that appears depends on the type of diagram you added.

● The graphic border surrounding the diagram will not print.

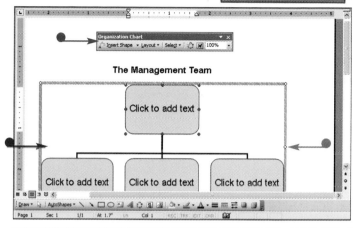

ADD TEXT TO THE DIAGRAM

6 Click in a shape of the diagram where you want to add text.

● A border surrounds that portion of the diagram.

7 Type the text you want to add.

Note: You can format the text you type the same way you format any text. See Chapter 5 for details.

8 Repeat steps **1** to **2** for each portion of the diagram.

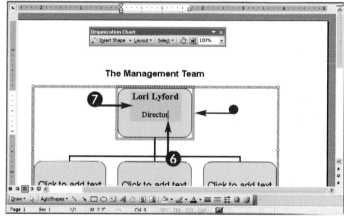

When should I use the various types of diagrams?

Organization charts show how chart elements are related and ranked. Pyramid diagrams show how diagram elements build on each other. Cycle diagrams illustrate procedures with uninterrupted cycles. Venn diagrams identify areas of similarity between diagram elements. Radial diagrams show how diagram elements relate to a central element. Target diagrams show progression toward a goal.

I added a diagram, but I cannot see it. Why not?

Word displays diagrams only in Print Layout, Web Layout, or Reading Layout views. Click the **Print Layout**, the **Web Layout**, or the **Reading** icon to change views.

continued

To keep your diagrams current and interesting, you can add or delete shapes and apply styles to diagrams.

Work with Diagrams *(continued)*

ADD OR DELETE SHAPES

① Click the shape above or beside where you want to add a shape.

● A border surrounds the shape you clicked.

② Click **Insert Shape**.

● To add a shape to an organization chart, click 🔽 beside **Insert Shape** and select the option that describes where the shape should appear.

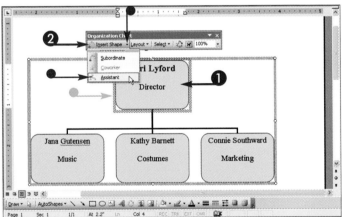

● The new shape appears.

● You can add text to the new shape by following the steps in the subsection "Add Text to the Diagram" on the previous page.

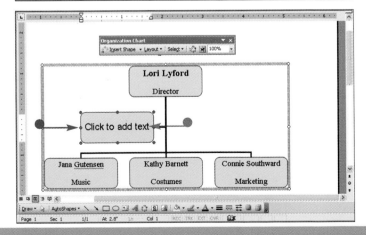

APPLY A DIAGRAM STYLE

1 Click the diagram so that handles (⬜) surround it.

2 Click the **AutoFormat** icon (🔲) on the diagram toolbar.

The Style Gallery dialog box appears and displays a list of available styles.

3 Click a style.

● A preview of the selected style appears here.

4 Click **OK**.

● Word applies the selected style to the diagram.

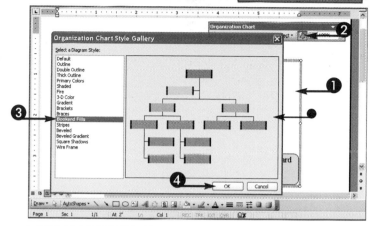

How can I delete a shape?
Click an edge of the shape; handles (⬛) appear around the shape. Press the Delete key to remove the selected shape from the diagram.

How can I remove a diagram style?
You cannot actually remove a diagram style; instead, you can simply use the default diagram style. Follow steps **1** to **4** in the subsection "Apply a Diagram Style" on this page, clicking **Default** in step **3**.

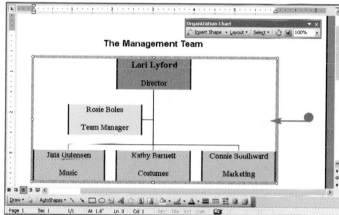

Customize Word

Do you like the default Word settings? If not, you can easily customize portions of the Word program to make it perform more in line with the way you work.

Display Formatting Marks

You can display formatting marks that do not print but help you identify formatting in your document.

Word can display formatting marks that represent spaces, tabs, paragraphs, hidden text, and optional hyphens.

① Open any document.

② Click the **Show/Hide** icon (¶).

Word displays all formatting marks in your document.

● Single dots (·) appear each time you press Spacebar; paragraph marks (¶) appear each time you press Enter; arrows (→) appear each time you press Tab.

● Hidden text appears underlined with dots.

● Optional hyphens, inserted by pressing Ctrl +-, appear as ¬.

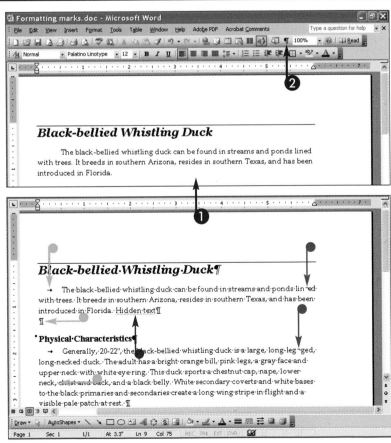

230

Control the Display of Formatting Marks

To more clearly view your document, you can limit the formatting marks that Word displays.

Control the Display of Formatting Marks

1 Click **Tools**.

2 Click **Options**.

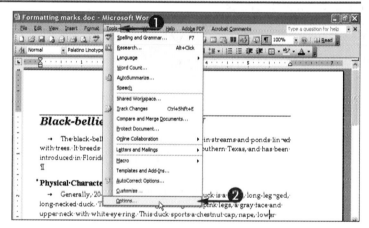

The Options dialog box appears.

3 Click the **View** tab.

4 Click the **All** option (☐ changes to ☑).

5 Click the formatting marks you want to display (☐ changes to ☑).

6 Click **OK**.

Word displays only the selected formatting marks in your document.

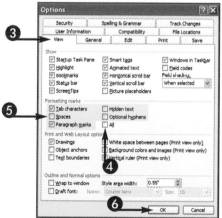

Add Buttons to a Toolbar

You can customize a toolbar by adding buttons to give yourself quick access to the commands you use most often.

Add Buttons to a Toolbar

1 If the toolbar you want to customize is not already displayed, right-click any toolbar and click the toolbar you want to customize to display it.

2 Click **Tools**.

3 Click **Customize**.

The Customize dialog box appears.

4 Click the **Commands** tab.

5 Click the category containing the button you want to add to a toolbar.

● The commands available in the selected category to add as buttons appear here.

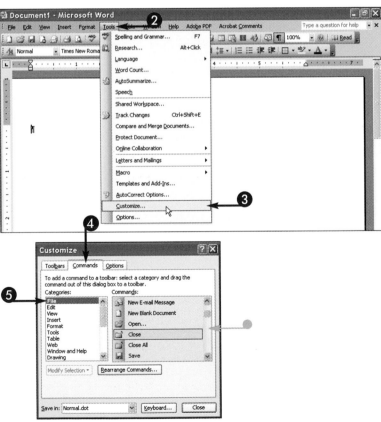

6 Drag the command you want to add to the toolbar.

● The mouse pointer changes to ▚, and ⊞ represents the location on the toolbar where the button will appear.

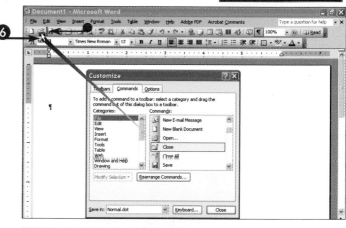

● The button appears on the toolbar.

7 Repeat steps **5** to **6** for each button you want to add.

8 Click **Close**.

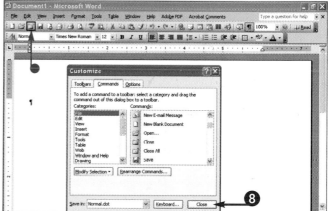

 TIP

Is there an easy way I can get rid of changes I made to a toolbar?

Yes, you can reset it, by following these steps:

1 Perform steps **1** to **3**.

2 Click the **Toolbars** tab.

3 Click the toolbar you want to restore to its original appearance.

4 Click **Reset**.

5 In the Reset Toolbar dialog box, click **OK**.

6 Click **Close**.

Word resets your toolbar.

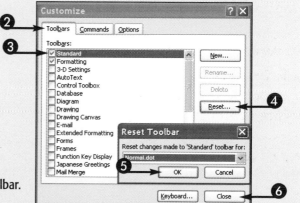

Rearrange Buttons on a Toolbar

You can move buttons around on a toolbar to make the toolbar work more effectively for you.

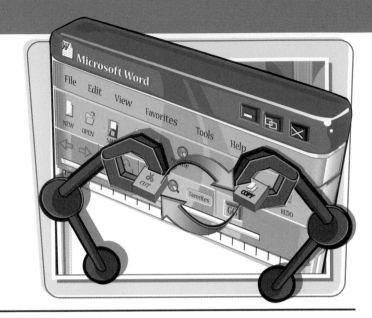

Rearrange Buttons on a Toolbar

① If the toolbar you want to customize is not already displayed, right-click any toolbar and click the toolbar you want to customize.

② Move the mouse pointer (⬚) over the button you want to move.

③ Press and hold **Alt** as you drag the button to a new location.

● The mouse ⬚ changes to ⬚, and ⬚ represents the button's position on the toolbar.

● The button appears in the new location on the toolbar.

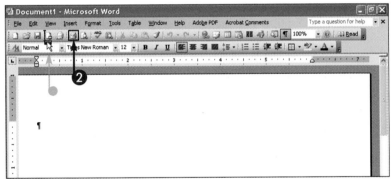

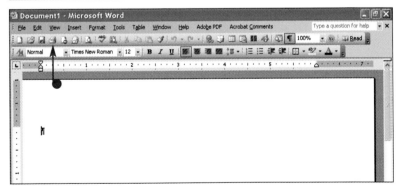

Remove Buttons from a Toolbar

You can remove buttons altogether from a toolbar to make the toolbar more functional for your work habits.

Remove Buttons from a Toolbar

① If the toolbar you want to customize is not already displayed, right-click any toolbar and click the toolbar you want to customize.

② Move the mouse ⬎ over the button you want to move.

③ Press and hold **Alt** as you drag the button off the toolbar.

● The mouse ⬎ changes to ⬎.

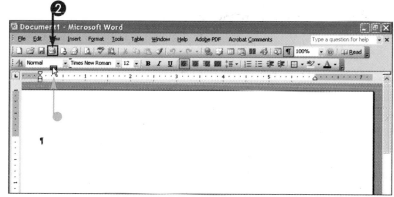

● The button disappears from the toolbar.

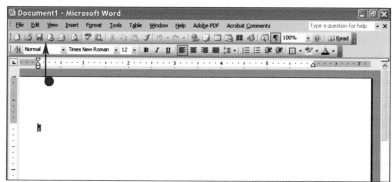

Create a New Toolbar

You can create a new toolbar that contains buttons you use on a regular basis.

You can, for example, create your own version of the Standard toolbar and then display your version instead of the original Standard toolbar.

Create a New Toolbar

1 Click **Tools**.

2 Click **Customize**.

The Customize dialog box appears.

3 Click the **Toolbars** tab.

4 Click **New**.

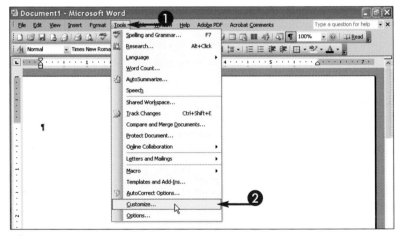

The New Toolbar dialog box appears.

⑤ Type a name for the toolbar.

⑥ Click **OK**.

● The new toolbar appears on-screen.

You can customize the toolbar to meet your needs by adding buttons to it.

Note: For more on adding buttons, see the section *"Add Buttons to a Toolbar."*

⑦ When you finish adding buttons to the toolbar, click **Close**.

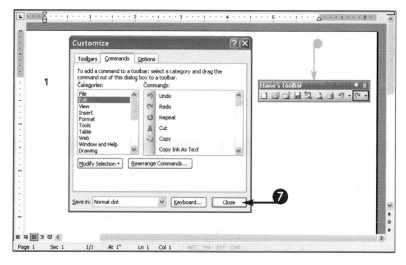

 TIPS

How can I hide the Standard toolbar and display my toolbar?

Before performing step **7**, click the **Toolbars** tab and click the box beside Standard to deselect it (☑ changes to ☐). The Standard toolbar disappears from view but your toolbar remains visible.

How can I make my toolbar appear where the Standard toolbar used to appear?

Drag your toolbar so that it appears just below the menu bar. Word will dock the toolbar automatically where the Standard toolbar used to appear.

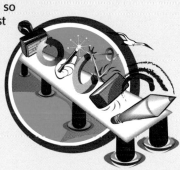

Add Commands to a Menu

You can add commands to menus to make them readily accessible when you need them.

① Click **Tools**.

② Click **Customize**.

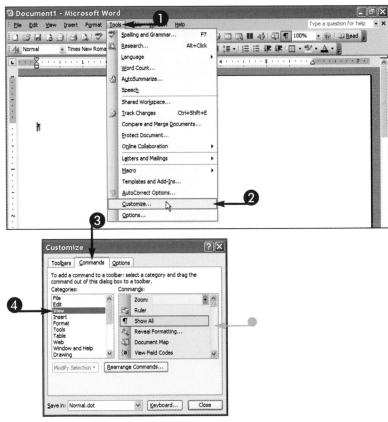

The Customize dialog box appears.

③ Click the **Commands** tab.

④ Click the category containing the command you want to add to a menu.

● The commands available in the selected category appear here.

5 Drag the command you want to add to a menu.

6 When the menu opens, position the mouse ⬚⬚ where you want the command to appear.

● The wide line represents the location on the menu where the command will appear.

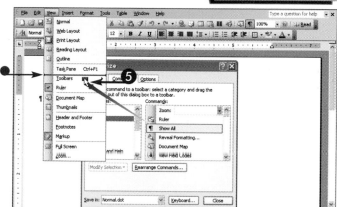

● The command appears on the menu.

7 Repeat steps **5** to **6** for each command you want to add.

8 Click **Close**.

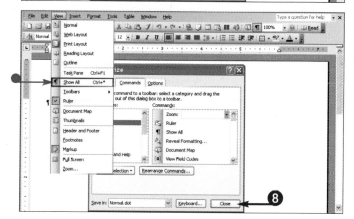

TIP

How can I add or change the letter I press on the keyboard to execute a menu command?

The hot key — the key you press to execute a menu command — is the underlined key on the menu.

1 In the Customize dialog box, right-click the command.

2 In the Name box, move the ampersand (&) so that it appears just before the letter you want to use as the hot key.

3 Click **Close**.

Word saves the change.

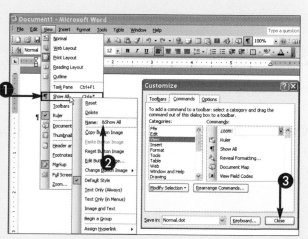

Rearrange Menu Commands

You can move menus and commands to different locations.

Using the technique described in this section, you can move commands to different positions on the same menu or to different menus. You also can move menus to different positions on the menu bar.

① Complete steps **1** to **2** in the section "Add Commands to a Menu" to display the Customize dialog box.

② Open the menu containing the command you want to move and move ⍓ over the command.

③ Drag the command to a new location.

The mouse ⍓ changes to ⍓.

● The wide line represents the command's position on the menu.

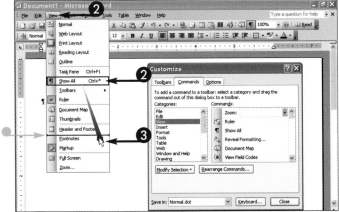

● The command appears in the new location on the menu.

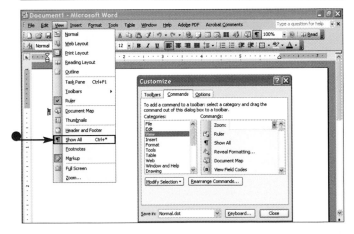

You can remove commands that you do not use from menus.

You can remove entire menus using the technique described in this section.

Remove a Command from a Menu

① Complete steps **1** to **2** in the section "Add Commands to a Menu" to display the Customize dialog box.

② Open the menu containing the command you want to remove and move the mouse ⩶ over the command.

③ Drag the command off the menu. The mouse ⩶ changes to ⩶ .

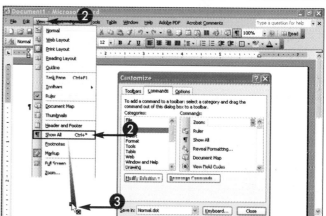

● The command disappears from the menu.

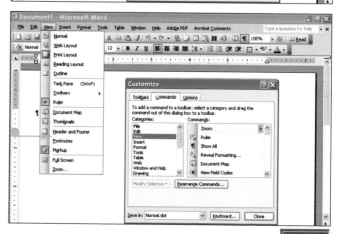

Create a New Menu

You can create a new menu that contains commands of your choice.

Creating a new menu can be useful when you have a group of commands that you use frequently.

Create a New Menu

① Click **Tools**.

② Click **Customize**.

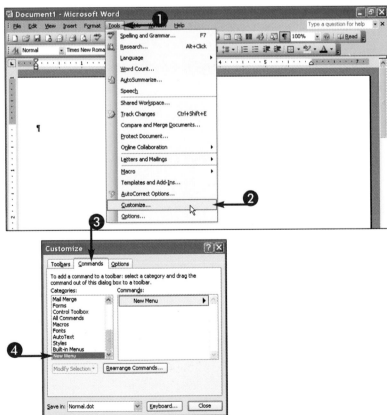

The Customize dialog box appears.

③ Click the **Commands** tab.

④ Click **New Menu** in the Categories list.

5 From the Commands list, drag New Menu to the location on the menu bar where you want the new menu to appear.

● The mouse ▷ changes to ▷⊞.

● The vertical line indicates the position of the new menu on the menu bar.

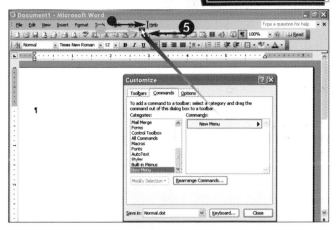

● The new menu appears in the selected location.

6 Right-click the new menu to display a submenu.

7 Type a name for the menu here. Include an ampersand (&) before the letter you want to use to open the menu by pressing **Alt** and then the letter.

You can add commands to the menu using the steps in the section "Add Commands to a Menu."

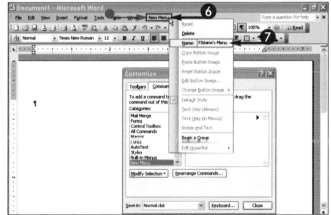

 TIPS

What does the Begin a Group command on the submenu enable me to do?

You can add lines to menus to group commands together. For example, on the submenu, a group ends before the Name command and another group begins immediately after the Name command.

What should I do if I change my mind and do not want the menu I created?

You delete the menu using the steps in the section "Remove a Command from a Menu."

Create a Macro

You can create a macro to save time. A macro combines a series of actions into a single command. For example, you can store in a macro repetitive text that you type frequently so that you can insert it quickly and easily.

You create a macro by recording the keystrokes you use to take the action you want to store in the macro.

1 Click **Tools**.

2 Click **Macro**.

3 Click **Record New Macro**.

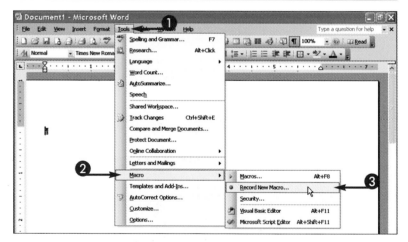

The Record Macro dialog box appears.

4 Type a name for the macro.

● The default description for the macro appears here.

● You can add to the description or type a different description for the macro.

⑤ Click **Keyboard** to assign the macro to a keyboard shortcut.

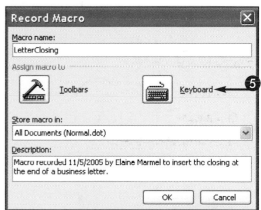

continued

TIPS

Are there any rules I should follow when naming a macro?

Macro names must begin with a letter and contain no spaces. In addition, if you think you may want to view the macro code, you may find it easiest to locate the macro if you name the macro something meaningful to you.

Can I assign a macro to a toolbar button?

Yes. In step **5**, click **Toolbars** instead of Keyboard. The Customize dialog box appears. Drag the macro from the Commands list to a toolbar. See the section "Add Buttons to a Toolbar" for details. You can rename the toolbar button by right-clicking it and changing the information in the Name box. Then, complete steps **8** to **10** on the pages that follow.

Create a
Macro *(continued)*

By assigning the macro to a keyboard shortcut, you can quickly and easily run the macro.

The Customize Keyboard dialog box appears.

6 Press and hold the **Alt** key and press a letter or number.

● The current assignment for the key combination you selected appears here.

If anything other than [unassigned] appears, press **Backspace** and repeat step **6** using a different key combination.

7 Click **Assign**.

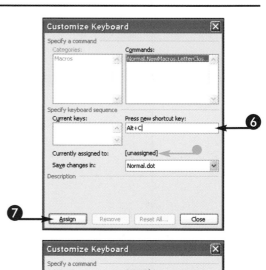

● The key combination appears here.

8 Click **Close**.

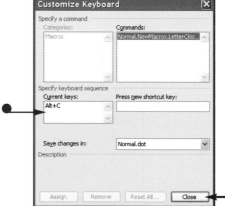

- The Stop Recording toolbar appears.

- REC appears in the status bar.

- The mouse ⅓ changes to ⅓ .

9 Perform the actions you want included in the macro.

Note: Macros can include typing, formatting, and menu or toolbar commands. You cannot use the mouse to position the insertion point.

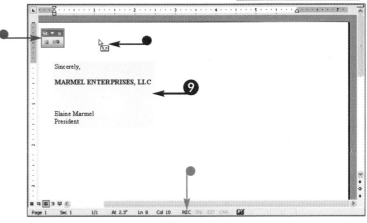

- You can click the **Pause Recording** icon (ⅰⅰ◑) to temporarily stop recording and then click the icon again to resume recording.

10 Click the **Stop Recording** icon (▣) when you have taken all the actions you want included in the macro.

Word saves the macro, the Stop Recording toolbar disappears, and REC disappears from the status bar.

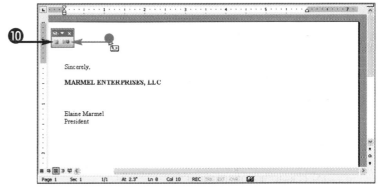

How can I view the macro code?

Follow these steps:

1 Perform steps **1** to **3** in this section, clicking **Macros** in step **3**.

2 In the Macros dialog box that appears, click the macro.

3 Click **Edit**.

- The macro code appears in a Visual Basic window.

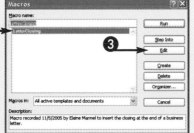

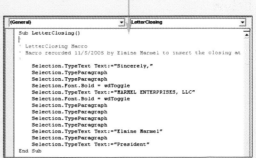

Run a Macro

You can run a macro to save time and let Word perform the actions stored in the macro.

To record a macro, see the section "Create a Macro."

Run a Macro

FROM THE MENUS

1 Position the insertion point in your document where you want the results of the macro to appear.

2 Click **Tools**.

3 Click **Macro**.

4 Click **Macros**.

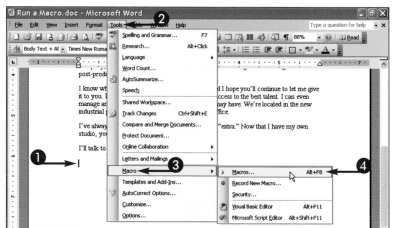

The Macros dialog box appears.

● Available macros appear here.

5 Click the macro you want to run.

● The macro's description appears here.

6 Click **Run**.

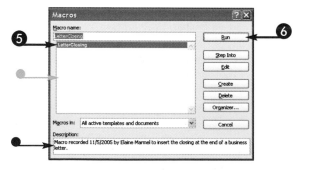

● Word performs the actions stored in the macro.

In this example, the macro inserted a closing for a business letter.

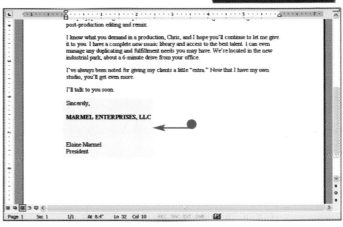

FROM A KEYBOARD SHORTCUT

❶ Position the insertion point in your document where you want the results of the macro to appear.

❷ Press the key combination you assigned to the macro.

● Word performs the actions stored in the macro.

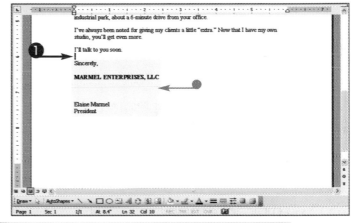

Can I assign a macro to a toolbar button after creating the macro?

Yes. To do so, perform these steps:

❶ Follow steps **1** to **4** in the section "Add Buttons to a Toolbar."

❷ In the Customize dialog box that appears, click **Macros** in the Categories list.

❸ Click and drag the macro from the Commands list to the toolbar.

● You can rename the button by right-clicking the toolbar button and typing a new name in the Name box.

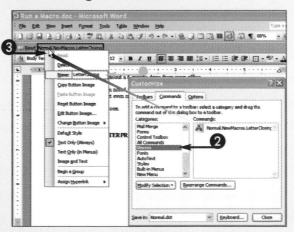

Work with Mass Mailing Tools

Why do the work yourself? You can use Word's mass mailing tools to create and mail form letters.

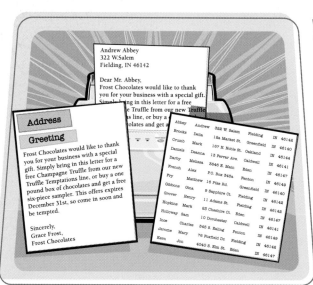

Using a form letter and a mailing list, you can quickly and easily create a mass mailing that merges the addresses from the mailing list into the form letter.

Typically, the only information that changes in the form letter is the addressee information. You can create the mailing list as you create the mass mailing, or you can use a mailing list that exists in another Word document or an Excel file.

1 Open a Word or an Excel file that you want to use as a mailing list.

This example uses an Excel file.

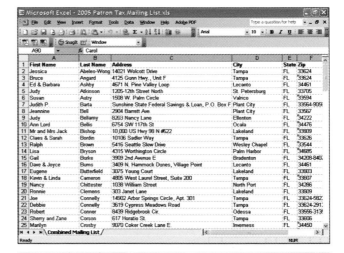

2 Open the Word document that you want to use as the form letter.

Note: The letter should not contain any information that will change from letter to letter, such as the inside address.

3 Click **Tools**.

4 Click **Letters and Mailings**.

5 Click **Mail Merge**.

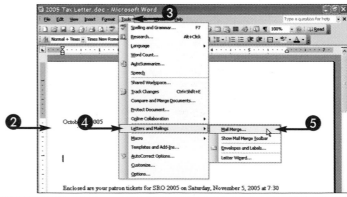

The Mail Merge task pane appears.

6 Click the **Letters** option (○ changes to ●).

7 Click the **Next: Starting document** link.

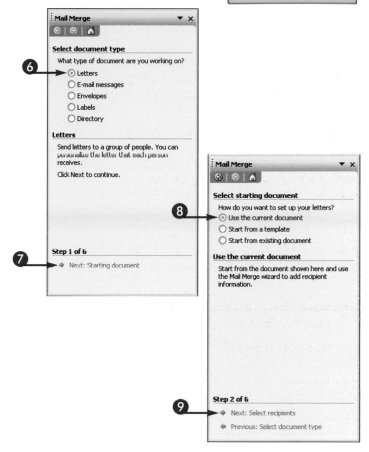

8 Click the **Use the current document** option (○ changes to ●).

9 Click the **Next: Select recipients** link.

continued

What should I do if I do not have an Excel file containing a mailing list?

Do not worry. Word enables you to use an existing file containing a mailing list as a convenience to you. If you do not have a file containing a mailing list, you will have the opportunity to create a mailing list as you walk through the mail merge process.

What format must a mailing list file I create in Excel follow?

Each row — called a *record* — must contain all the information about a single letter recipient. Each column — called a *field* — must contain a single piece of information such as the recipient's first name. If you do not have a first name for one recipient, leave that cell blank. Column names should contain no spaces.

For the mailing list, you can use an existing mailing list stored in either a Word or an Excel document.

This section uses a mailing list stored in Excel.

Select recipients

○ **Use an existing list**

○ ...t from Outlook contacts

○ ...e a new list

Create Letters to Mass Mail *(continued)*

⑩ Click the **Use an existing list** option (○ changes to ⦿).

⑪ Click the **Browse** link.

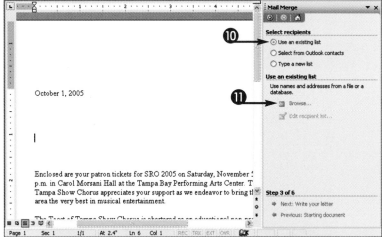

The Select Data Source dialog box appears.

⑫ Click the **Look in** ⬇ to navigate to the folder containing the mailing list.

● You can use these buttons to navigate to commonly used folders.

⑬ Click the file containing the mailing list.

⑭ Click **Open**.

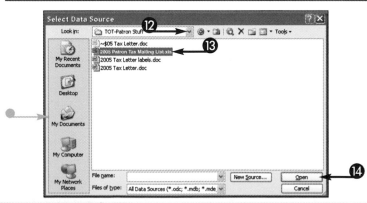

When you select an Excel file, the Confirm Data Source dialog box appears.

⑮ Click **MS Excel Worksheets via DDE (*.xls)**.

⑯ Click **OK**.

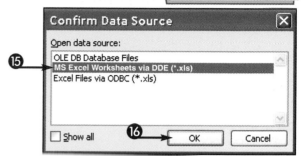

After a pause, while Word links with Excel, the Microsoft Excel dialog box appears.

Note: *During the pause, watch the status bar in Word to view the actions happening to link the files.*

⑰ Click **OK**.

Note: *If the Excel notebook contains multiple sheets, you can select a specific sheet in the Microsoft Excel dialog box.*

If I do not have a mailing list in another file, how do I create one?

To create a mailing list, follow these steps:

❶ In step **9**, click the **Type a new list** option (○ changes to ◉).

❷ In the middle of the Mail Merge task pane, click the **Create** link.

❸ In the New Address List window, type address information and click **New Entry**.

The **Cancel** button changes to the **Close** button.

❹ Repeat step **3** for each addressee.

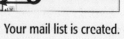

❺ When you finish, click **Close**.

❻ Save your Address List and skip to step **18** in this section.

Your mail list is created.

continued

You can select specific recipients from the
mailing list to receive the form letter, and
you use a merge field to specify the place
in your document where the recipient's
address should appear.

After another short pause, while Excel and Word
complete the link, the Mail Merge Recipients
dialog box appears.

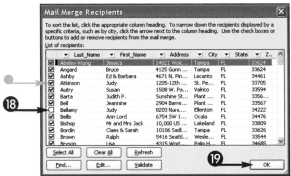

● A check mark (☑) appears beside each
person's name, identifying the recipients of the
form letter.

⑱ Click beside any addressee to whom you do not
want to mail a form letter (☑ changes to ☐).

⑲ Click **OK**.

● The name of the file containing the mailing list
appears here.

● You can drag the left edge of the Mail Merge
task pane to widen the pane and view the entire
file name.

⑳ Click the **Next: Write your letter** link.

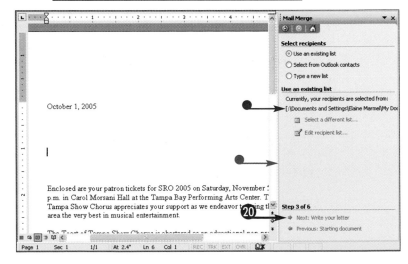

㉑ Click the location where you want the inside address to appear in the form letter.

㉒ Click the **Address block** link.

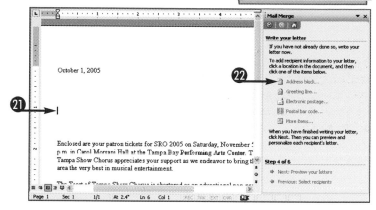

The Insert Address Block dialog box appears.

㉓ Click a format for each recipient's name.

● You can preview the format here.

● You can use these boxes to add other options to the inside address.

㉔ Click **OK**.

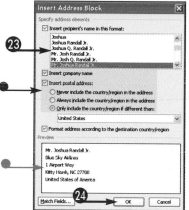

How do I know that Word will assign the correct fields in my mailing list file to the recipient's address information?

To make sure that Word assigns the correct fields, follow these steps:

❶ After you complete step **23**, click **Match Fields**.

The Match Fields dialog box appears.

❷ Beside each required field, click the ⊡ and select the corresponding field name in your mailing list file.

❸ Click **OK** and continue with step **24**.

Word matches your fields.

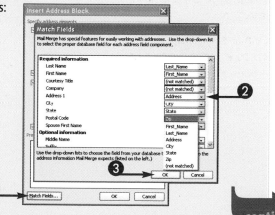

continued

You can use a merge field to
provide a greeting line in your
letter and you can preview the
merged letter results.

Create Letters to Mass Mail *(continued)*

● A merge field representing the address block in
the letter appears.

*Note: When you complete the merge, Word replaces the merge
field with name and address information from your address file.*

㉕ Click in the location where you want the
greeting to appear.

㉖ Click the **Greeting line** link.

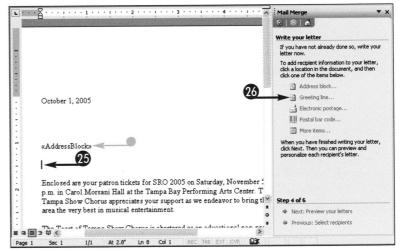

The Greeting Line dialog box appears.

㉗ Click the 🔽 beside these boxes to specify the
greeting format.

● A preview of the greeting appears here.

● You also can specify a greeting for addresses
that do not conform to the typical layout of
names and addresses.

㉘ Click **OK**.

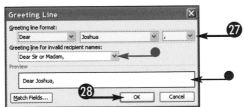

- A merge field appears in the letter.

Note: *When you complete the merge, Word replaces the merge field with greeting information.*

29 Click the **Save** icon (🖫) to save the changes to the letter.

30 Click the **Next: Preview your letters** link.

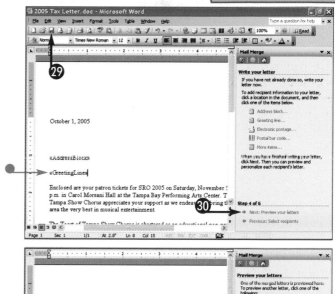

- Word displays a preview of the merged letter, using the unchanging content of the letter and information from the address file.

- You can click the **Right arrow** icon (>>) to preview the next letter and the **Left arrow** icon (<<) to move back and preview the previous letter.

31 Click the **Next: Complete the merge** link.

Can I add other changing information to a form letter?

Yes, as long as your mailing list contains fields — column headings — for the other changing information you want to include.

1 Position the insertion point in the letter where a field should appear.

2 Click the **More Items** link.

3 From the Insert Merge Field window that appears, click the field you want to insert.

4 Click **Insert**.

Word inserts a merge field for the field you selected.

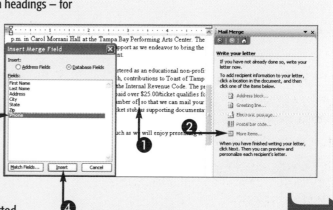

continued

After you finish adding merge fields, you can select specific recipients or simply create one letter for each person in the mailing list file.

Create Letters to Mass Mail *(continued)*

Word is ready to combine the form letter information with the mailing list file information.

32 Click the **Edit individual letters** link.

The Merge to New Document dialog box appears.

33 Click an option to identify the recipients of the letter (⚪ changes to ⦿).

The **All** option creates a letter for all entries on the mailing list; the **Current record** option creates only one letter for the recipient whose letter you are previewing; the **From** option creates letters for recipients you specify.

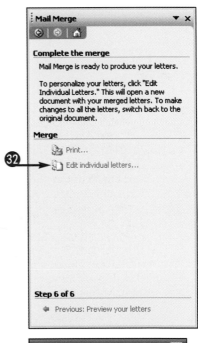

● If you selected **From** in step **33**, click here to type the first and last record numbers for the people to whom you want to send the letter.

34 Click **OK**.

● Word merges the form letter information with the mailing list information in a new Word document named Letters1.

The new document contains individual letters for each mailing list recipient.

35 Click the **Print** icon (🖨) to print the letters.

● You can click 🖫 and assign a new name to save the merged letters.

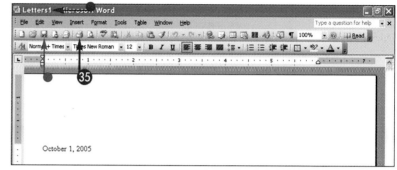

Must I create a separate document containing the individual letters to print them?

No. You can print them from the Complete the merge pane of the Mail Merge task pane. In step **32**, click **Print** instead of Edit individual letters.

How do I know what numbers to supply if I click From in the Merge to New Document dialog box?

If you used an Excel file, you can open the file in Read-Only mode and identify the first and last row numbers. If you created the list during the merge process, you can use the Preview your letters pane and click ⊳⊳ and ⊲⊲ to determine the first and last record numbers.

1	Abbey	An...
2	Brooks	Delia
3	Crumb	Mark
4	Daniels	Deanna
5	Darby	Melissa
6	French	Alex
7	Fry	Matth...
8	Gibbons	Gir...

Create Labels for a Mass Mailing

In addition to creating personalized form letters for a mass mailing, you can use the merge feature to create mailing labels for each mass mailing recipient.

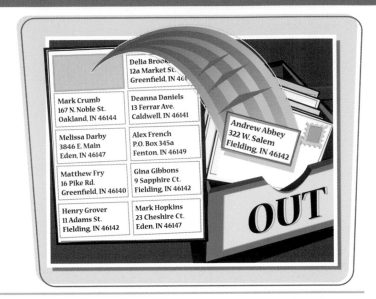

① Click **Tools**.

② Click **Letters and Mailings**.

③ Click **Mail Merge**.

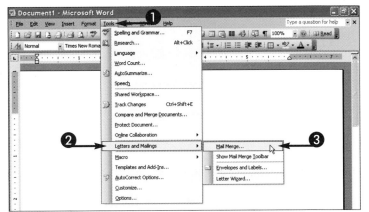

The Mail Merge task pane appears.

④ Click the **Labels** option (○ changes to ◉).

⑤ Click the **Next: Starting document** link.

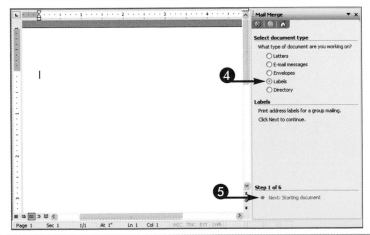

6 Click the **Change document layout** option (○ changes to ●).

7 Click the **Label options** link.

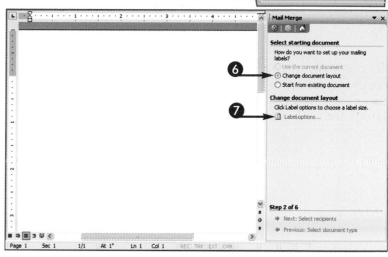

The Label Options dialog box appears.

8 Click an option to select the type of printer (○ changes to ●).

9 Click ▼ to select a label product.

10 Click the label's product number.

● Information about the label dimensions appears here.

11 Click **OK**.

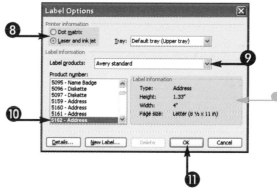

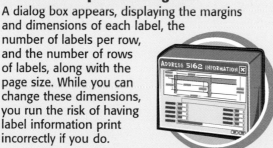

TIPS

What happens if I click Details in the Label Options dialog box?

A dialog box appears, displaying the margins and dimensions of each label, the number of labels per row, and the number of rows of labels, along with the page size. While you can change these dimensions, you run the risk of having label information print incorrectly if you do.

What happens if I click New Label in the Label Options dialog box?

A dialog box appears. Word bases the appearance of this dialog box on the settings selected in the Label Options dialog box. You can use this dialog box to create your own custom label. Type a name for the label and then adjust the margins, height and width, number across or down, vertical or horizontal pitch, and page size as needed.

continued

Using the label options you specify, Word sets up a document of labels to which you add merge information.

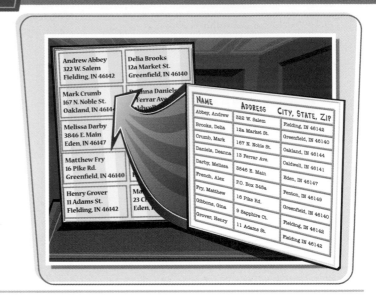

Create Labels for a Mass Mailing *(continued)*

● Word sets up the document for the labels you selected.

⑫ Click the **Next: Select recipients** link.

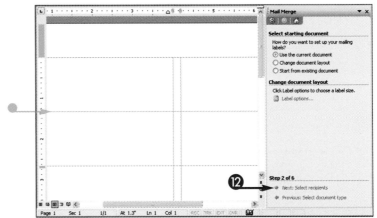

⑬ Click **Type a new list** (○ changes to ◉).

⑭ Click the **Create** link.

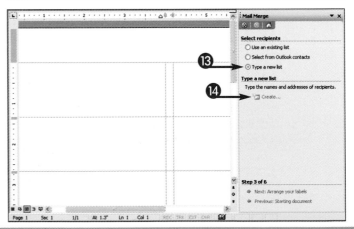

The New Address List window appears.

⑮ Type information for the first recipient in these boxes.

⑯ Click **New Entry**.

⑰ Repeat steps **15** to **16** for each recipient.

⑱ Click **Close**.

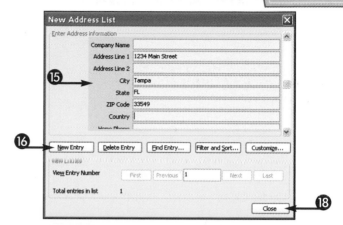

The Save Address List window appears.

● If necessary, click ⊠ or use the buttons to navigate to the folder where you want to save the mailing list file.

⑲ Type a name for the mailing list file.

⑳ Click **Save**.

If I already have a mailing list file set up, can I use it?

Yes. Simply follow these steps:

❶ In step **13**, click the **Use an existing list** option (○ changes to ◉).

❷ Click the **Browse** link.

❸ Using the Select Data Source dialog box that appears, navigate to the location of the mailing list file.

❹ Click **Open**.

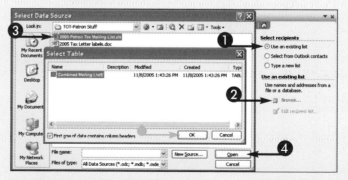

● If the file is an Excel workbook, click the type of Data Source in the Select Table dialog box and click **OK**. Then, select the appropriate sheet.

When the Mail Merge Recipients dialog box appears, continue with step **21**.

continued

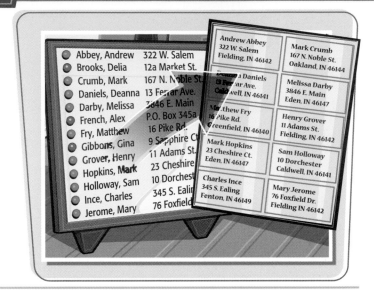

You can create labels for only some of
the recipients in the mailing list file.
You set up the first label to include the
merge fields you want on all labels.

The Mail Merge Recipients dialog box appears.

A check box (☑) appears beside each person's
name, identifying the recipients of the form letter.

㉑ Click beside any addressee to whom you do not
want to mail a form letter (☐ changes to ☑).

㉒ Click **OK**.

㉓ Click the **Next: Arrange your labels** link.

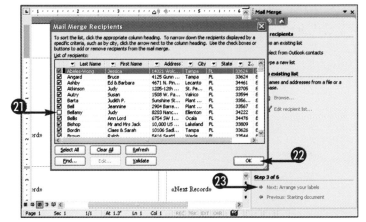

You Set up the first label to include the merge fields
used for all labels.

㉔ Click the first label where you want the first merge
field to appear.

㉕ Click the **Address block** link.

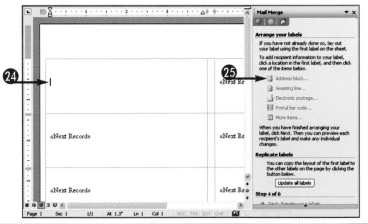

The Insert Address Block dialog box appears.

㉖ Click a format for each recipient's name.

● You can preview the format here.

● You can use these boxes (☐ changes to ☑) to add other options to the inside address.

㉗ Click **OK**.

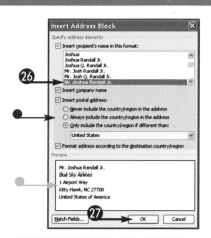

● Word adds the merge field to the first label.

Note: When you complete the merge, Word replaces the merge field with information from the mailing address file.

㉘ Click **Update all labels**.

㉙ Click the **Next: Preview your labels** link.

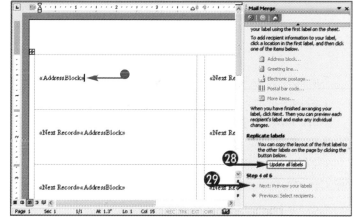

TIP

I cannot see the Next: Preview your labels link; what am I doing wrong?

Nothing. You need to scroll down in the Mail Merge task pane. When you position the mouse pointer (⯭) over the down arrow (▼) at the bottom of the Mail Merge task pane, the Mail Merge task pane shifts downward and ▼ disappears. You can then shift the Mail Merge task pane contents upward by moving the mouse ⯭ over the upward-pointing arrow (▲) at the top of the task pane.

continued

You can preview the labels before you print them. When you complete the merge, you can merge all records in the mailing list file or only those you select.

● Word displays a preview of one page of labels, replacing the merge field with information from the mailing list file.

● You can click >> to preview the next label and << to move back and preview the previous label.

㉚ Click the **Next: Complete the merge** link.

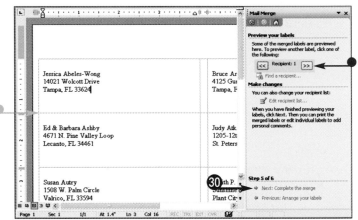

Word is ready to produce the labels.

㉛ Click the **Edit individual labels** link.

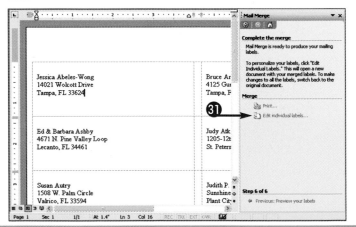

The Merge to New Document dialog box appears.

32 Click an option to identify the recipients of the letter (⚪ changes to ⚫).

The **All** option creates a letter for all entries on the mailing list; the **Current record** option creates only one letter for the recipient whose letter you are previewing; the **From** option creates letters for recipients you specify.

33 Click **OK**.

● Word creates the labels in a new Word document named Labels1.

● The new document contains individual labels for each mailing list recipient.

34 Click to print the labels.

The labels print.

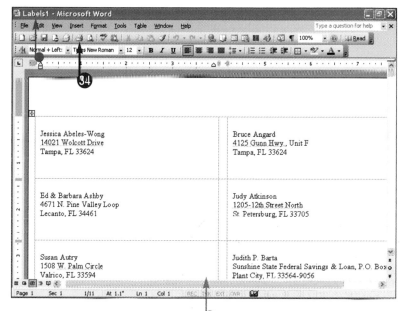

What happens if I click Print on the Complete the merge pane?

The Merge to Printer dialog box appears. After you select the records you want to print, Word merges the information, allows you to select a printer, and then prints the merged label information without creating a separate document. This approach is useful if you know you do not need to make any changes to the labels.

If I merge to a document, should I save it?

Because you can re-create the merge whenever you need the labels, saving is not necessary. However, if you expect to print the labels often, you can save time if you save the labels.

Work with Speech Recognition

Using the Speech Recognition feature, you can enter and format text in Word documents and operate menus, toolbars, and dialog boxes using your voice.

Set Up Speech Recognition

You can enter information into a Word document and select commands from menus, toolbars, and dialog boxes using your voice. To use this feature, you must set up speech recognition on your computer.

Make sure that you connect a microphone and speakers to your computer to use this feature. Setting up speech recognition involves adjusting your microphone and training Office to understand your voice.

Set Up Speech Recognition

① Click **Tools**.

② Click **Speech**.

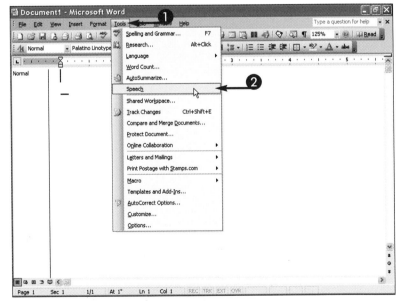

A message appears explaining that speech recognition files are not currently installed.

③ Click **Yes** to install the Speech Recognition feature.

When the installation process finishes, the Welcome to Office Speech Recognition wizard appears.

④ Click **Next**.

Welcome to Office Speech Recognition

To increase the accuracy and reliability of speech recognition, you must first:
1. Adjust your microphone.
2. Train Office for speech recognition.
This will take about 15 minutes. Please make sure you are in a quiet environment. Click Next to begin the training process.

④ Next > Cancel

The Microphone Wizard – Welcome dialog box appears.

● Instructions for positioning a headset microphone appear here.

⑤ Click **Next**.

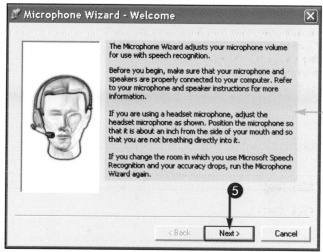

Microphone Wizard - Welcome

The Microphone Wizard adjusts your microphone volume for use with speech recognition.

Before you begin, make sure that your microphone and speakers are properly connected to your computer. Refer to your microphone and speaker instructions for more information.

If you are using a headset microphone, adjust the headset microphone as shown. Position the microphone so that it is about an inch from the side of your mouth and so that you are not breathing directly into it.

If you change the room in which you use Microsoft Speech Recognition and your accuracy drops, run the Microphone Wizard again.

⑤ < Back Next > Cancel

TIPS

Can I completely control Word using speech recognition?

The Speech Recognition feature is not intended to be used exclusively. Instead, you will find that you work most efficiently if you use a combination of speech recognition, keyboard strokes, and mouse clicks.

Are there special requirements I must have to use speech recognition?

Yes. Your computer's processor should be at least 400 MHz and your computer should have at least 128 MB of memory and be using Windows 2000 Service Pack 3 or Windows XP Service Pack 2. You should use a high-quality close-talk microphone; typically, a headset microphone will work best.

continued

Set Up Speech Recognition *(continued)*

As part of setting up the Speech Recognition feature, you need to set the volume and position of your microphone.

6 Read this sentence aloud.

● The volume meter displays the volume of your voice through the microphone.

7 Repeat step **6**, monitoring the volume level as you read.

8 When the volume level remains consistently in the green range, click **Next**.

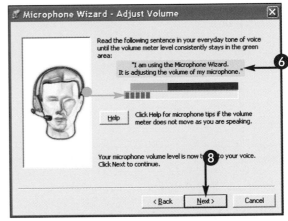

The Microphone Wizard – Test Positioning dialog box appears.

9 Read this sentence aloud.

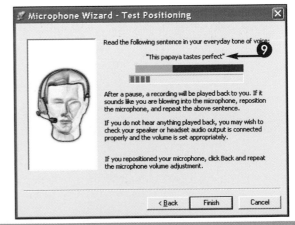

After a pause, you hear a recording of your voice playing back to you.

If the recording sounds like you are blowing into the microphone, reposition the microphone and repeat step **9**.

If you reposition the microphone, click Back and complete steps **6** to **9** again.

⑩ Click **Finish**.

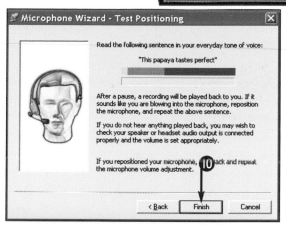

The Voice Training wizard begins.

● The text in this area explains that you must complete at least one voice training session to use the Speech Recognition feature.

⑪ Click **Next**.

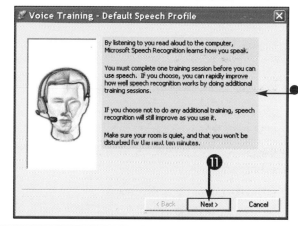

Why are the volume and position of my microphone important?

The Speech Recognition feature works best when you use it consistently. By establishing a standard microphone volume, you are less likely to encounter errors where speech recognition indicates you spoke too softly or too loudly. Using a consistent microphone position helps ensure that the Speech Recognition feature understands you.

Is there any significance to the sentence that I read to adjust the microphone position?

The sentence "This papaya tastes perfect" contains explosive consonants. Using a sentence containing explosive consonants helps the Speech Recognition feature adjust its interpretation of your speech, making it more likely to understand you.

As the last portion of setting up the Speech Recognition feature, you train Microsoft Office Word 2003 to understand your speaking style.

Set Up Speech Recognition *(continued)*

● This text explains how to train the Speech Recognition feature to understand your voice.

⑫ Click **Sample**.

You hear a sample of how you should speak during the training session.

⑬ Click **Next**.

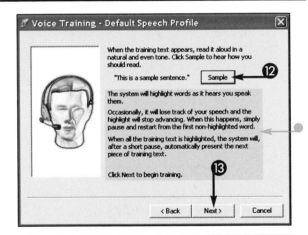

● Sample text appears.

⑭ Read the text.

● As you read, the Voice Training wizard highlights the words it recognizes.

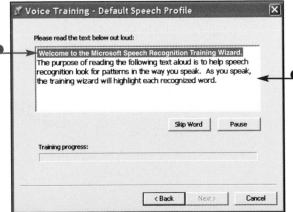

When you finish reading the sample text, the Voice Training wizard automatically displays the next box in the wizard.

The Voice Training wizard continues to display a series of boxes containing text for you to read.

⑮ Read the text in each box as it appears.

● You can click **Pause** to take a break during training. To resume, click the **Resume** button that appears in place of the **Pause** button.

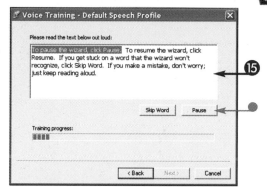

When you finish reading the last box of text, this window appears.

⑯ Click **Finish**.

Note: *The Office Speech Training Video appears in a browser window. When the video finishes, click the **Close** icon (✕) to close the window.*

● The Language toolbar appears at the top of the Word window. You can use this toolbar to perform speech recognition tasks.

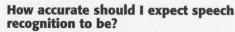
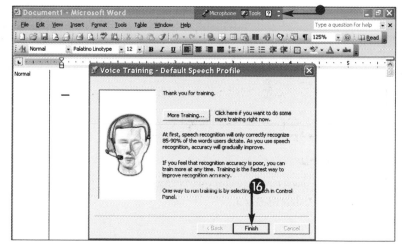

TIPS

Should I speak in any special way during speech training?

You should read the boxes presented to you during training in as smooth and consistent fashion as possible. Do not slow down your speaking habits or leave pauses between words. Do not read faster than you typically speak. Read naturally.

How accurate should I expect speech recognition to be?

After you complete the initial training, speech recognition should recognize 85–90 percent of the words you dictate. The more you use the feature, the more accurate it will become. If you do not achieve results in line with these estimates, consider doing more training. Click **Tools** on the Language toolbar and then click **Training**.

Work in Dictation Mode

You can use Dictation Mode to enter text into a Word document by speaking into your microphone.

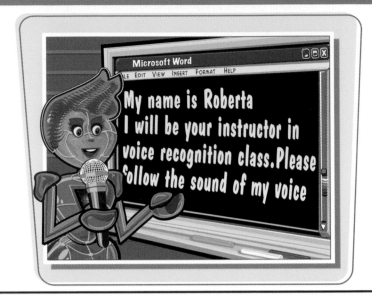

Work in Dictation Mode

1 Click **Microphone** on the Language toolbar to turn on your microphone.

● The Dictation and Voice Command buttons appear on the Language toolbar.

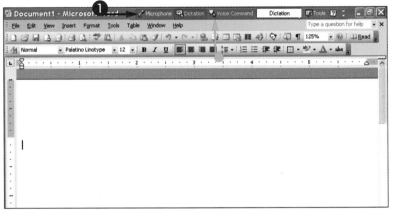

2 Click or say **Dictation**.

3 Say the words you want to appear in your document into the microphone.

● As you speak, a light blue bar appears, indicating that speech recognition is evaluating your speech.

You can continue speaking while the light blue bar appears.

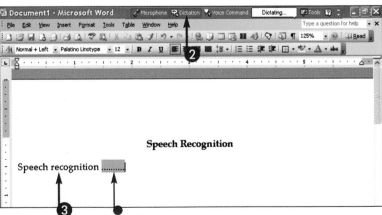

● Eventually, the words you say replace the light blue bar.

● You can include punctuation by saying the name of the punctuation mark you want to include.

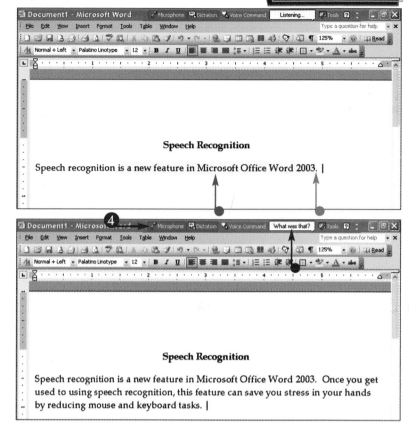

● Tips and status messages appear here.

These tips and status messages can help improve the accuracy of the speech recognition feature.

④ When you finish dictating, click or say **Microphone**.

TIPS

I keep saying a word and speech recognition does not seem to understand; is there some way to force it to understand?

Yes. With your microphone on, click **Tools** on the Language toolbar and then click **Add/Delete Word(s)**. In the Add/Delete Word(s) window, type the word you want to record; then, click **Record pronunciation** and say the word. When speech recognition finishes recording, the word appears in the Dictionary list.

If I make a mistake while dictating, what should I do?

You can say "Backspace" repeatedly to have Word delete the characters, from right to left, of the last word you said. Speech recognition understands the names of most of the keys on your keyboard; for example, you can say "Enter" to begin a new paragraph.

Work in Voice Command Mode

You can use Voice Command mode to issue verbal commands that you do not want to appear as part of your text. For example, you can save your document or open a different document.

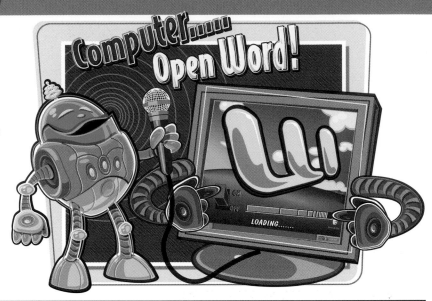

TURN ON VOICE COMMAND MODE

1 If your microphone is off, click **Microphone**.

● The microphone is on if the Dictation and Voice Command buttons appear on the Language toolbar.

2 Click or say **Voice Command**.

● The message area displays Voice Command to indicate the mode you are using.

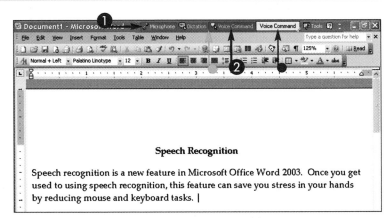

ISSUE MENU COMMANDS

3 Say the name of the menu containing the command; for example, say **Tools**.

● The menu opens and the menu name appears in the message area.

4 Say the name of the command you want to use.

To close a menu without saying a command, you can say **Escape**.

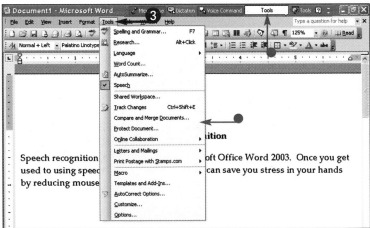

ISSUE TOOLBAR BUTTONS

5 Say the name of the toolbar button.

● Word performs the action of the button.

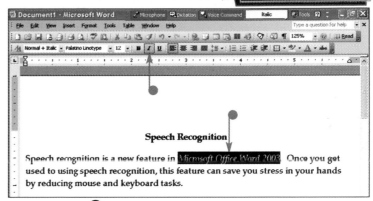

Speech Recognition

Speech recognition is a new feature in *Microsoft Office Word 2003*. Once you get used to using speech recognition, this feature can save you stress in your hands by reducing mouse and keyboard tasks.

ISSUE DIALOG BOX OPTIONS

6 Say the name of the option; for example, say **Small caps**.

● To switch tabs in a dialog box, say the name of the tab you want to use.

7 Say **OK** to save your selections.

8 Turn off the microphone by saying or clicking **Microphone**.

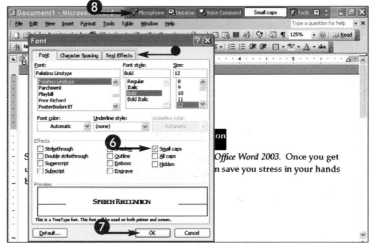

 TIPS

Suppose that I want to use a toolbar button but I do not know its name. How do I determine the button's name?

To identify the name of the toolbar button, point the mouse (⦶) over the button; a ScreenTip appears showing the button name.

ScreenTip

Can I say "Microphone" to turn the microphone on?

No, you cannot. When the microphone is off, Microsoft Office Word does not recognize any voice commands, including the command to turn on the microphone.

14

Word and the Internet

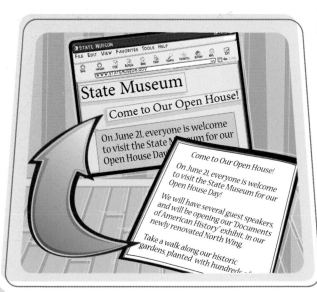

Using Word, you can interact with others over the Internet. You can e-mail a document, create a hyperlink in a document that will open a Web page or another document at your own site, and you can save a document as a Web page.

E-mail a Document

You can e-mail a Word document while you work in Word; you do not need to open your e-mail program and send the document from there.

Although you do not need to send the document from your e-mail program, your e-mail program must be set up on your computer.

E-mail a Document

1 Open the document you want to send by e-mail.

2 Click the e-mail icon (📧).

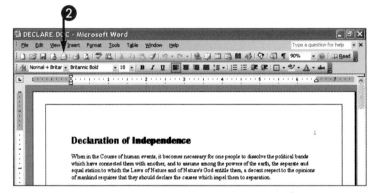

● Word adds an area where you can address the e-mail.

3 Click here to type the e-mail address of the person to whom you want to send the document.

● You can type the e-mail address of someone to whom you want to send a copy of the message.

Note: To send the message, or copies of the message, to multiple recipients, separate each e-mail address with a semi-colon (;) and a space.

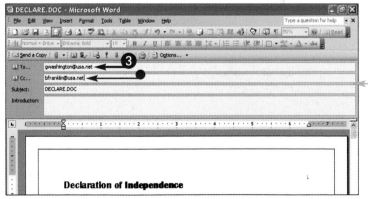

284

④ Click here to type a subject for the e-mail message.

Note: Subjects are not required but including one is considerate. Word automatically supplies the document name for the subject; you can replace the document name with anything you want.

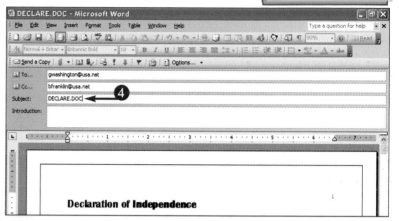

● If you use Microsoft Outlook as your e-mail program, you can click here to include an introduction for the document.

⑤ Click **Send a Copy**.

Word places a message in your e-mail program's Outbox and removes the e-mail address area from the top of the screen.

Note: Your e-mail program must be open for the message to be sent.

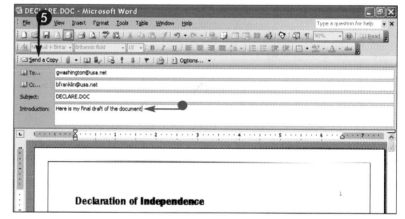

What should I do if I change my mind and do not want to send the document as an e-mail message?

Repeat step **2**; Word removes the area from the top of the document where you address the e-mail message.

Does Word send my document as an attachment?

If you use the method described in these steps, Word displays the document in the body of an e-mail message. To send the document as an attachment, open the document. Then, click **File**, click **Send To**, and then click **Mail Recipient (as Attachment)**. A standard e-mail window appears, with the document appearing as an attachment. Complete steps **3** to **5**.

Create a Hyperlink

Using a hyperlink, you can connect a word, phrase, or graphic image in a Word document to another document on your computer or in your company's network, or to a Web page on the Internet.

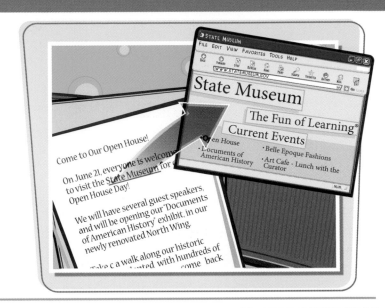

Create a Hyperlink

1 Select the text or graphic you want to use to create a hyperlink.

2 Click **Insert**.

3 Click **Hyperlink**.

● You can click the **Insert Hyperlink** icon (📄) instead of performing steps **2** to **3**.

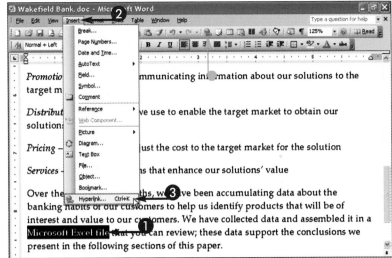

The Insert Hyperlink dialog box appears.

4 Click **Existing File or Web Page**.

● Files in the current folder appear here.

5 Click here and navigate to the folder containing the document to which you want to link.

6 Click the file to select it.

7 Click **ScreenTip**.

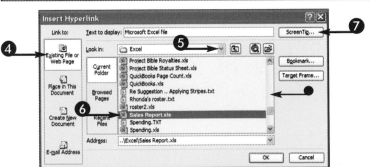

The Set Hyperlink ScreenTip dialog box appears.

8 Type text that should appear when a user moves the mouse ⌶ over the hyperlink.

9 Click **OK**.

The Insert Hyperlink dialog box reappears.

10 Click **OK**.

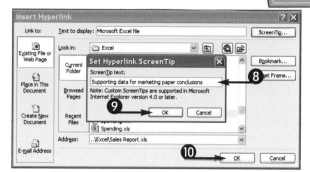

● Word creates a hyperlink shown as blue, underlined text in your document.

● The ScreenTip text appears when you move the mouse ⌶ over the hyperlink.

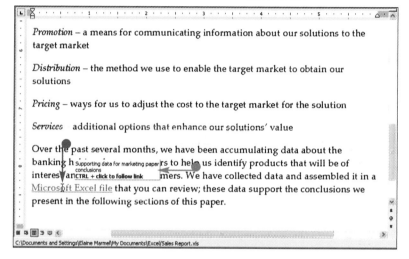

Promotion – a means for communicating information about our solutions to the target market

Distribution – the method we use to enable the target market to obtain our solutions

Pricing – ways for us to adjust the cost to the target market for the solution

Services   additional options that enhance our solutions' value

Over the past several months, we have been accumulating data about the banking h̲ Supporting data for marketing paper conclusions rs̲ to help us identify products that will be of interest anCTRL + click to follow link mers. We have collected data and assembled it in a Microsoft Excel file that you can review; these data support the conclusions we present in the following sections of this paper.

C:\Documents and Settings\Elaine Marmel\My Documents\Excel\Sales Report.xls

TIPS

If I do not create a ScreenTip for the hyperlink, what appears when I place ⌶ over the hyperlink?

Word displays the location on your computer's hard disk or in your network, or, if you linked to a Web page, Word displays the Web address.

How do I use a hyperlink that appears in a Word document?

Press and hold **Ctrl** as you click the hyperlink. The linked document or Web page will appear.

Save a Document as a Web Page

You can save any Word document as a Web page that you can then upload to the Internet.

Save a Document as a Web Page

1 Open the document you want to save as a Web page.

2 Click **File**.

3 Click **Save as Web Page**.

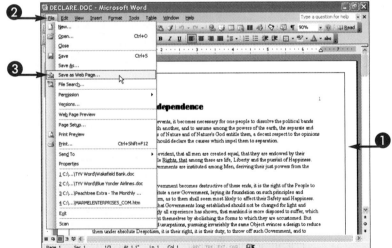

The Save As dialog box appears.

4 Type a file name for the Web page here.

● The location where Word will save the file appears in the Save in dialog box; you can click ▼ to save the Web page in a different location.

● You can use these icons to navigate to commonly used locations.

5 Click **Change Title**.

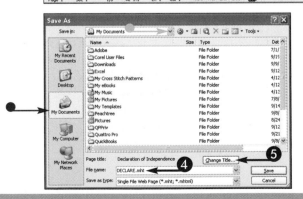

The Set Page Title dialog box appears.

6️⃣ Type the title that you want to appear at the top of the screen when the page is displayed in a Web browser.

7️⃣ Click **OK**.

The Save As dialog box reappears.

8️⃣ Click **Save**.

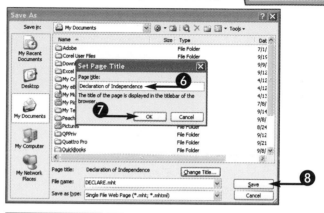

● Word saves the document as a Web page and displays the document in Web Layout view, showing the document as it will appear in a Web browser.

Declaration of Independence

When in the Course of human events, it becomes necessary for one people to dissolve the political bands which have connected them with another, and to assume among the powers of the earth, the separate and equal station to which the Laws of Nature and of Nature's God entitle them, a decent respect to the opinions of mankind requires that they should declare the causes which impel them to separation.

We hold these truths to be self-evident, that all men are created equal, that they are endowed by their Creator with certain Unalienable Rights, that among these are life, Liberty and the pursuit of Happiness. That to secure these rights, governments are instituted among Men, deriving their just powers from the consent of the governed,

That whenever any form of Government becomes destructive of these ends, it is the right of the People to alter or to abolish it and to institute a new Government, laying its foundation on such principles and organizing its power in such form, as to them shall seem most likely to affect their Safety and Happiness. Prudence, indeed, will dictate that Governments long established should not be changed for light and transient causes; and accordingly all experience has shown, that mankind is more disposed to suffer, while evils are sufferable, than to right themselves by abolishing the forms to which they are accustomed. But when a long train of abuses and usurpations, pursuing invariably the same Object evinces a design to reduce them under absolute Despotism, it is their right, it is their duty, to throw off such Government, and to provide new Guards for their future security.

Such has been the patient sufferance of these colonies; and such is now the necessity which constrains them to alter their former Systems of Government. The history of the present King of Great Britain is a history of repeated injuries and usurpations, all having in direct object the establishment of an absolute Tyranny over these States. To prove this, let Facts be submitted to a candid world.

TIP

After I close the Web page, what should I do if I want to reopen it?

Follow these steps:

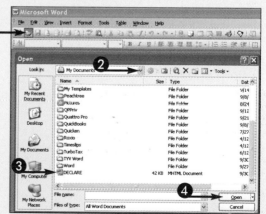

1️⃣ Click the **Open** icon (📄).

2️⃣ In the Open dialog box that appears, click here and navigate to the folder where you saved the Web page.

3️⃣ Click the Web page document, which displays a special Microsoft Word icon (📰).

4️⃣ Click **Open**.

Word reopens the Web page.

Index

Symbols and Numbers

& (ampersand) for menu command hot key, 239
[ ] (brackets) surrounding bookmarked text, 51
- (minus sign) in Document Map, 58
three-dimensional styles for graphics, 221

A

address lists. *See* mailing lists
aligning text
    in columnar fashion, 7
    indenting paragraphs, 114–115
    in paragraph, 108
    in table cells, 196
    vertically on page, 144
    wrapping around graphics, 222–223
ampersand (&) for menu command hot key, 239
antonyms, finding for words, 84–85
Article on Microsoft Online icon, 15
attachments to e-mail, sending documents as, 285
AutoComplete feature
    AutoText and, 79
    described, 7
AutoCorrect dialog box
    AutoCorrect tab, 76–77
    Smart Tags tab, 65
AutoCorrect feature
    changing back corrections, 77
    correcting mistakes automatically, 76–77
    smart tags, 64–65
    stopping a specific correction, 77
AutoCorrect Options icon, 77
AutoShapes
    adding, 212–213
    adding shadows, 220
    changing colors, 218
    deleting, 213
    moving, 216, 217
    resizing, 217
    rotating, 219
    three-dimensional, 221
AutoText feature, 78–79

B

backup copies of documents
    opening, 27
    saving, 23
Basic File Search task pane, 34–35
Behind text wrapping style, 223
blank lines, inserting, 46
boldface text
    applying, 98
    finding and replacing, 73
Bookmark dialog box, 50
bookmarks, 9, 50–51
borders
    around pages, 164–165
    around paragraphs, 118–119
    around table cells, 198–199
Borders and Shading dialog box
    Borders tab, 118–119
    Page Border tab, 164–165
    Shading tab, 120–121

brackets ([ ]) surrounding bookmarked text, 51
Break dialog box
    inserting column breaks, 169
    inserting page breaks, 140–141, 159
    inserting section breaks, 146–147
breaks
    column, 169
    line, 46
    page, 140–141, 159
    section, 146–147
bulleted lists, 112–113
Bullets and Numbering dialog box, 112–113

C

case, changing for selected text, 100
cells of tables
    adding borders, 198–199
    aligning text in, 196
    combining, 194
    defined, 185
    removing borders, 199
    shading, 197
    splitting, 195
centering text, 108
Change Case dialog box, 100
character styles, 133. *See also* styles
charts. *See* diagrams
clip art
    collections, 211
    copying to clipboard, 209
    finding images, 208–209, 211
    inserting, 208–210
    moving, 216, 217
    resizing, 217
    rotating, 219
Clip Art task pane, 208, 210, 211
Clipboard task pane, 53, 209
closing. *See also* stopping
    documents, 33
    Find and Replace dialog box, 51
    Header and Footer toolbar, 152
    Help window, 15
    menu using speech recognition, 280
    task pane, 12
    Word, 4
collections of clip art, 211
colors
    for borders around paragraphs, 119
    changing for graphics, 218
    changing for selected text, 101
    highlighting text, 102
    for shading paragraphs, 120–121
column breaks, 169
Columns dialog box, 168–169
columns of tables
    adding, 192
    changing width, 187
    deleting, 193
    fitting to longest item, 187
    splitting cells into, 195
columns of text. *See* newspaper columns

Index

dictionaries
 adding words to the spelling dictionary, 81
 for Translation feature, 66
disabling grammar and spell checking, 82–83
displaying. *See* viewing or displaying
document area, 5
Document Map, 58, 59
dot leader tabs, 117
double spacing. *See* line spacing
dragging and dropping
 buttons to a toolbar, 232–233
 changing table column width, 187
 changing table row height, 186, 187
 commands to a menu, 238–239
 rearranging buttons on a toolbar, 234
 rearranging menu commands, 240
 removing buttons from a toolbar, 235
 removing commands from a menu, 241
 tables, moving, 188
 tables, resizing, 189
 text, 53
 toolbars, 237
drawing
 AutoShapes, 212–213
 hiding the drawing canvas, 213, 215
 text boxes, 214–215
Drawing toolbar
 AutoShapes icon, 212
 Shadow icon, 220
 Text Box icon, 214
 3-D Style icon, 221

E

Edit menu
 Clear submenu, 104
 Copy command, 53
 Cut command, 53
 Find command, 70
 Office Clipboard command, 53, 209
 Paste command, 53
 Replace command, 72
 Select All command, 49
Edit WordArt dialog box, 205
editing. *See also* formatting paragraphs; formatting text
 adding to existing text (inserting), 42
 checking spelling and grammar, 80–81
 copying text between documents, 54–55
 copying text within a document, 52–53
 correcting formatting inconsistencies, 123
 correcting mistakes automatically, 76–77
 deleting text, 44–45
 Document Map for navigating, 58
 document views for, 56–57
 endnotes, 158–159
 finding synonyms or antonyms, 84–85
 footnotes, 158–159
 inserting blank lines, 46
 inserting symbols, 62–63
 marking and finding your place, 50–51
 moving text between documents, 54–55
 moving text within a document, 52–53

pictures, 207
 in Print Preview window, 173
 in protected documents, 38–39
 replacing text by overwriting, 42
 reviewing tracked changes, 92–93
 searching and replacing text, 72–73
 searching for text, 70–71
 selecting text, 48–49
 smart tags for, 64–65
 table of contents and, 161
 tracking changes, 39, 90–91
 translating text to another language, 66–67
 undoing changes, 47
 viewing thumbnails of pages, 59
 WordArt, 205
 zooming in or out, 60
e-mailing documents, 284–285
embedding fonts in saved documents, 23
enabling grammar and spell checking, 83
endnotes. *See* footnotes or endnotes
Enter key
 AutoComplete feature and, 7
 inserting a line break, 46
 starting a new paragraph, 6, 46
entering text
 adding comments to a document, 88–89
 AutoComplete feature, 7
 bulleted lists, 113
 in diagrams, 225, 226
 for envelopes, 178, 179
 inserting (adding to existing text), 42
 inserting frequently used text automatically, 78–79
 insertion point and, 6
 for labels, 181
 numbered lists, 113
 replacing by overwriting, 43
 separating information with tabs, 6
 starting a new paragraph, 6
 in table cells, 185
 in text boxes, 215
Envelope Options dialog box, 179
Envelopes and Labels dialog box
 Envelopes tab, 178–179
 Labels tab, 180–181
envelopes, printing, 178–179
erasing. *See* deleting or removing
Excel
 mailing list files, 252, 253, 254–255, 261, 265
 Merge to New Document dialog box and, 261

F

Factiva iWorks fee-based search engine, 87
fields in mailing lists, 253, 257
File menu
 Close command, 33
 File Search command, 34
 New command, 28
 Open command, 24, 26
 Page Setup command, 138, 144, 145, 150, 176
 Print command, 91
 Print Preview command, 172

Index

Index

Index

Index

Index

Read Less–Learn More®

There's a Visual book for every learning level...

Simplified®

The place to start if you're new to computers. Full color.

- Computers
- Mac OS
- Office
- Windows

Teach Yourself VISUALLY™

Get beginning to intermediate-level training in a variety of topics. Full color.

- Computers
- Crocheting
- Digital Photography
- Dreamweaver
- Excel

- Guitar
- HTML
- Knitting
- Mac OS
- Office

- Photoshop
- Photoshop Elements
- PowerPoint
- Windows
- Word

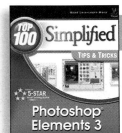

Top 100 Simplified® Tips & Tricks

Tips and techniques to take your skills beyond the basics. Full color.

- Digital Photography
- eBay
- Excel
- Google

- Internet
- Mac OS
- Photoshop

- Photoshop Elements
- PowerPoint
- Windows

Build It Yourself VISUALLY™

Do it yourself the visual way and without breaking the bank. Full color.

- Game PC
- Media Center PC

...all designed for visual learners—just like you!

Master VISUALLY®

Step up to intermediate-to-advanced technical knowledge. Two-color interior.

- 3ds max
- Creating Web Pages
- Dreamweaver and Flash
- Excel VBA Programming
- iPod and iTunes
- Mac OS
- Optimizing PC Performance
- Photoshop Elements
- QuickBooks
- Quicken
- Windows Server
- Windows

Visual Blueprint™

Where to go for professional-level programming instruction. Two-color interior.

- Excel Data Analysis
- Excel Programming
- HTML
- JavaScript
- PHP

Visual Encyclopedia™

Your A to Z reference of tools and techniques. Full color.

- Dreamweaver
- Photoshop
- Windows

For a complete listing of Visual books, go to wiley.com/go/visualtech

Visual
An Imprint of ⊕WILEY
Now you know.

Want instruction in other topics?

Check out these
All designed for visual learners—just like you!

For a complete listing of *Teach Yourself VISUALLY*™ titles and other Visual books, go to wiley.com/go/visualtech

Visual®
An Imprint of ⊕WILEY
Now you know.

Wiley, the Wiley logo, the Visual logo, Read Less-Learn More, and Teach Yourself Visually are trademarks or registered trademarks of John Wiley & Sons, Inc. and/or its affiliates. All other trademarks are the property of their respective owners.